W9-AFH-999

One Flew Over the Cuckoo's Nest

Rising to Heroism

Twayne's Masterwork Studies
Robert Lecker, General Editor

One Flew Over the Cuckoo's Nest

Rising to Heroism

M. Gilbert Porter

TWAYNE PUBLISHERS • BOSTON
A Division of G. K. Hall & Co.

One Flew Over the Cuckoo's Nest: Rising to Heroism
M. Gilbert Porter

Twayne's Masterwork Studies No. 22

Copyright 1989 by G. K. Hall & Co.
All rights reserved
Published by Twayne Publishers
A Division of G. K. Hall & Co.
70 Lincoln Street
Boston, MA 02111

Book production by Gabrielle B. McDonald
Copyediting supervised by Barbara Sutton
Typeset in 10/14 Sabon
by Compset, Inc., of Beverly, Massachusetts

Printed on permanent/durable acid-free paper
and bound in the United States of America

Library of Congress Cataloging-in-Publication Data

Porter, M. Gilbert.
    One flew over the cuckoo's nest : rising to heroism / M. Gilbert
Porter.
        p.   cm. — (Twayne's masterwork studies ; no. 22)
    Bibliography: p.
    Includes index.
    ISBN 0-8057-7988-4 (alk. paper). ISBN 0-8057-8037-8 (pbk. : alk.
paper)
        1. Kesey, Ken. One flew over the cuckoo's nest.   I. Title.
II. Series.
PS3561.E6670537 1988
813.54 — dc19   88-13104
                                                                  CIP

To
my son,
Phillip

We never know how high we are
Till we are called to rise
And then if we are true to plan
Our statures touch the skies—

The Heroism we recite
Would be a daily thing
Did not ourselves the Cubits warp
For fear to be a King—

—Emily Dickinson

CONTENTS

NOTE ON REFERENCES
AND ACKNOWLEDGMENTS

I am grateful to the Research Council of the University of Missouri—Columbia and to the UMC English department for the time and the funds necessary to complete this study. I am indebted for conscientious research assistance to both Patrick Gonder of the UMC English department and to Jeaneice Brewer of the UMC humanities library, for expert preparation of the typescript to Marilynn Keil and Dana Bennett of the UMC English department, for permission to reprint his photograph of Kesey to Wayne Eastburn of the *Eugene Register-Guard,* for helpful suggestions to improve the commentary on the historical context to my colleagues Bob Collins and Bob Sattelmeyer, and for consultation on songs and related matters to the folklorists Elaine Lawless and W. K. McNeil.

For permission to reprint copyrighted material, I am grateful to the following publishers: Ken Kesey and the Viking Press: From *One Flew Over the Cuckoo's Nest* by Ken Kesey. Copyright © 1962 by Ken Kesey. All rights reserved. Reprinted by permission of Viking Penguin Inc. Illustrations from *Kesey's Garage Sale* by Ken Kesey. Copy-

ONE FLEW OVER THE CUCKOO'S NEST

References to *One Flew Over the Cuckoo's Nest* are to the readily
available Signet paperback edition.

Photo by Wayne Eastburn, *Eugene Register-Guard*

CHRONOLOGY: KEN KESEY'S LIFE, WORKS, AND TIME

1935   Ken Elton Kesey is born 17 September in La Junta, Colorado,
              the son of dairy farmers Fred A. and Geneve (Smith) Kesey.
              An avid reader, Kesey lists among his youthful reading Edgar
              Rice Burroughs and Zane Grey, after whom he is to name his
              first son. Fred Kesey used to say of young Ken, "That boy
              could draw a crowd in a desert." Franklin D. Roosevelt is in
              the White House, and America is enduring the worst depres-
              sion of its national life.

1941   Nazi Germany threatens destruction of Europe and interna-
              tional Jewry; the Japanese bomb Pearl Harbor on 7 December,
              drawing America into full participation in World War II.

1945   America drops atomic bombs on Hiroshima and Nagasaki.
              The Potsdam Treaty facilitates the end of the war. Richard
              Wright publishes *Black Boy*.

1946–1953   After his discharge from the U.S. Navy, Fred Kesey moves his
              family to Springfield, Oregon, where he resumes dairy farming
              and is instrumental in forming the Eugene Farmer's Coopera-
              tive. Ken and his younger brother, Joe (known as "Chuck"),
              swim and fish in the streams and hunt in the lush forests of
              the Willamette Valley and the Cascade Mountains. Ken at-
              tends high school in Springfield, where he boxes, wrestles,
              plays guard on the football team, participates in Thespian ac-
              tivities, and is voted by his graduating class at Springfield High

"the most likely to succeed." In 1947 Jackie Robinson, Branch Rickey, and the Brooklyn Dodgers integrate major league baseball, and in the following year President Truman begins the integration of the armed services. In 1952 David Riesman publishes *The Lonely Crowd*, marking a decade of conformity dominated by "other-directed" rather than "inner-directed" people. Ralph Ellison publishes *Invisible Man*.

1953–1957　At the University of Oregon in Eugene, Kesey is an outstanding wrestler, an actor, an aspiring playwright, and a nondrinking member of Beta Theta Pi who is popular in the fraternity for his talent at writing skits, designing house decorations, and instigating pranks. Kesey credits James B. Hall as a major influence on his writing as an undergraduate. During the summers, Kesey does gofer work in Hollywood, and on 20 May 1956 he marries Faye Haxby, his high school sweetheart. A year later, he receives his bachelor's degree in speech and communications. In 1954 the Supreme Court declares segregation unconstitutional in the landmark case *Brown v. Board of Education*. Dwight D. Eisenhower begins the second term of his presidency, a period of quietness on campuses, the dominance of the organization man in the "gray flannel suit," and the growth of the beatnik resistance to conformity and materialism. Jack Kerouac publishes *On the Road*, which becomes the guidebook for the beat generation. His protagonist, Dean Moriarty, is based on Neal Cassady. Other counterculture writers are Lawrence Ferlinghetti, Gary Snyder, Gregory Corso, Bob Kaufman, John Clellan Holmes, and Allen Ginsberg. The City Lights Bookstore in San Francisco becomes homebase for the disenchanted.

1958　Kesey works a year, does bit parts in Hollywood films, and completes "End of Autumn," an unpublished novel about college sports.

1959–1961　Kesey enters the graduate writing program at Stanford University on a Woodrow Wilson Fellowship. There he studies with Malcom Cowley, Wallace Stegner, Richard Scowcroft, and, briefly, with Frank O'Connor. As the most colorful resident of Perry Lane, Kesey counts among his friends his fellow students and writers Ken Babbs, Wendell Berry, Larry McMurtry, Ed McClanahan, Gurney Norman, and Bob Stone. During the summer of 1960 Kesey writes a novel about San Francisco's North Beach entitled "Zoo," also unpublished. At the suggestion of psychology graduate student Vik Lovell, to whom *Cuckoo's Nest* is dedicated, Kesey becomes a volunteer for government drug experiments from the summer of 1960 to the spring of 1961, when he takes a job as a psychiatric aide in the veteran's hospital at Menlo Park. The twin experiences with drugs and patients prepare him for the writing of his first published novel. In June 1961, Kesey moves to Springfield, Oregon, to help Chuck expand the Springfield Creamery. On 20 January President John F. Kennedy is inaugurated, and Robert Frost recites "The Gift Outright" as an inaugural poem.

1962 Publication of *One Flew Over the Cuckoo's Nest.* Kesey moves to Florence on the Oregon coast to do research for his logging novel, riding with the local loggers to and from the woods in the "crummies," the crew trucks, and drinking in the bars where the loggers hang out. After four months, Kesey returns to Perry Lane.

1963 Kesey moves from Perry Lane to La Honda, where he finishes his second novel and establishes a base of operations for the friends, heads, and rock-music junkies who become the Merry Pranksters. The stage version of *Cuckoo's Nest* opens in New York on 14 November, with Kirk Douglas playing McMurphy. After unfavorable reviews, the play closes in three months. John F. Kennedy is assassinated in Dallas on 22 November. Lyndon Baines Johnson becomes president.

1964 *Sometimes a Great Notion* is published in July. Kesey has said of the autobiographical elements in the novel that he was writing in part to discover "which side of me really is: the woodsy, logger side—complete with homespun homilies and cracker-barrel corniness, a valid side of me that I like—or its opposition. The two Stamper brothers in the novel are each one of the ways I think I am." Kesey and Ken Babbs and the Merry Pranksters take their 1939 International Harvester school bus (for which Kesey paid $1,500) cross-country to "do drugs," see and be sights, and celebrate the publication of the novel. The destination sign on the bus reads "Furthur"; a sign on the back warns "Caution: Weird Load." The driver is Neal Cassady. The revelers record the trip on forty hours of film called simply "The Movie." "You're either on the bus or off the bus," say the Pranksters, and "You have to put other people in your movie or they will put you in theirs." Their film is often the centerpiece of Prankster presentations known as "acid tests," communal high jinks with LSD that serve socially as mind-mileage markers for the hippie movement in America.

1965 The Pranksters return to La Honda to edit "The Movie." Kesey is arrested in April for possession of marijuana and goes through a year of court hearings. He is convicted and files an appeal. On 7 August Kesey hosts an extended party in La Honda for the San Francisco branch of the Hell's Angels.

1966   Kesey is arrested on 19 January on a second possession charge. He flees to Mexico, continues to experiment with drugs—especially LSD—and with various forms of related "power," returns in the fall, is arrested again in October, is tried through two hung juries, and is eventually sentenced to and serves five months in the San Mateo County Jail and the San Mateo County Sheriff's Honor camp. *Life, Newsweek,* and other national magazines do stories on LSD, Congress makes the use of it illegal, and the FDA warns of dangerous side effects.

1967   Kesey is released in November.

1968   Kesey moves to the farm at Pleasant Hill, Oregon, where he completes work on his jail journals, *Cut the Mother-Fuckers Loose.* In February Neal Cassady, whom Kerouac called the "Holy Goof," dies in Mexico counting railroad ties. In August Tom Wolfe publishes *The Electric Kool-Aid Acid Test,* a new-journalistic account of the Merry Pranksters. Richard Nixon defeats Hubert Humphrey for president.

1969   Kesey lives from March to June in London, England, where he is involved with Apple Records in an unsuccessful project to record authors reading from their own work. He returns to the farm in Pleasant Hill and refuses to join the Pranksters in a trip to the Woodstock rock festival. When they return, they find a sign Kesey has erected in his driveway saying irrevocably "No." This sign marks both the disbanding of the Pranksters and a new period of stability in Kesey's life. "The biggest thing I've learned from dope," he says, "is that there are forces beyond human understanding that are influencing our lives."

1970   In the spring Kesey makes *Atlantis Rising,* an unreleased children's movie. During the summer Paul Newman's company films *Sometimes a Great Notion* for release the following year. In July Kesey's three-year probation is over.

1971   With Paul Krassner, Kesey edits *The Last Supplement to the Whole Earth Catalogue.*

1972   Nixon defeats George McGovern, winning a second term.

1973   Viking publishes *Kesey's Garage Sale,* which includes the screenplay *Over the Border,* a psychodramatic movie script based on Kesey's flight to Mexico. American troops are withdrawn from Vietnam after years of political turbulence and protests.

1974   Kesey begins a serial publication called *Spit in the Ocean* published by Intrepid Trips Information Service, a loosely organized group composed of Kesey and his friends. The first issue focuses on old people and includes Kesey's "The Thrice-Thrown Tranny Man or Orgy at Palo Alto High School" and part 1 of *Seven Prayers by Grandma Whittier*, whose octogenarian protagonist is modeled on Kesey's grandmother. During a trip to Egypt, Kesey publishes in *Rolling Stone* five dispatches between November 1974 and February 1975 on exploring the pyramids. Kesey and Babbs are instrumental in organizing The Bend in the River Council, an activist group interested in ecological issues. The Watergate scandal leads to Nixon's resignation (9 August) and the presidency of Gerald Ford.

1975   A film version of *One Flew Over the Cuckoo's Nest*, directed by Milos Forman, is released late in the year. Although it is a popular success, winning five Academy Awards, Kesey refuses to see the film, denounces the filmmakers for artistic tampering, and sues them for breach of contract, collecting a small out-of-court settlement in 1976. South Vietnam falls to the communists.

1976   In the March issue of *Esquire*, Kesey publishes "Abdul and Ebenezer," a largely autobiographical story about cattle raising in Oregon. *Spit in the Ocean* no. 2 is published, with the second part of *Seven Prayers*. Jimmy Carter defeats Gerald Ford for the presidency.

1977   *Spit in the Ocean*, no. 3 is published, with the third part of *Seven Prayers*.

1978   *Spit in the Ocean*, no. 4 is published, with the fourth part of *Seven Prayers*.

1979   "The Day after Superman Died," Kesey's tribute to Neal Cassady, appears in the October issue of *Esquire*. *Spit in the Ocean*, no. 5 is published, with "Search for the Secret Pyramid" and the fifth part of *Seven Prayers*.

1980   Ronald Reagan defeats Jimmy Carter for the presidency. The age of "yuppies" (Young Urban Professionals) is in full swing.

1981   Kesey goes to China to cover the Beijing Marathon. *Spit in the Ocean*, no. 6 appears, with the sixth part of *Seven Prayers*.

1982   Kesey's "Running into the Great Wall" is published in *Running*.

1984   Kesey's younger son, Jed, a wrestler like his father, is killed in the winter on a University of Oregon wrestling-team trip in a highway accident between Pendleton, Oregon, and Pullman, Washington. It is this son whom Kesey had breathed life back into after an auto-train wreck in Springfield, Oregon, in the late sixties, a moving incident recounted in the "Tools from My Chest" section of *The Last Supplement to the Whole Earth Catalogue*. Reagan is reelected with strong support from growing conservative groups.

1986   In August Viking publishes *The Demon Box*, mostly a collection of Kesey's previously published stories and essays. The dedication is "To Jed/ across the river/ riding point." In memory of his deceased son and as a hedge against a similar disaster in the future, Kesey donates a large new traveling van to the University of Oregon wrestling team. Kesey occasionally plumps for the book or enhances his readings or lectures with performances on what he calls his Thunder Machine, a 1962 Thunderbird converted into a flashy, self-resonating musical instrument. "I call it," he says, "a kind of Modern Jazz Quartet of Junk."

1987   Kesey has at least three creative projects in progress: 1) the concluding section of *Seven Prayers by Grandma Whittier*; 2) a film tentatively entitled "Last Go 'Round" about a black American Rodeo champion from 1911 named George Fletcher, his Indian companion named Jackson Sundown, and a white cowboy named John Spain; and 3) a novel set in Alaska with the working title "Sailor's Song," excerpts from which appeared in the November 1982 issue of *Life*. Kesey and his devoted wife, Faye, continue to live close to the animals and the land on the farm in Pleasant Hill. They have reared four children there: their sons, Zane and Jed, their daughter, Shannon, and Kesey's daughter by Mountain Girl (Carolyn Adams), Sunshine. The stock brand that Kesey uses is formed in the shape of a skeleton key above the letter Z, which, for humane reasons, he applies by a freezing process far less painful to animals than the conventional burning process. Will he stay on the farm? Kesey leaves no doubt: "I got a kid buried on this land. They'll have to get me off with a bulldozer."

1988   The Western Literature Association honors Kesey with its annual Award for Distinguished Achievement in Writing.

1

HISTORICAL CONTEXT

A European visitor to America in the 1980s concluded her guided tour of a midwestern city with this candid and trenchant observation: "It all looks so *temporary.*" What she had seen was a typical American cityscape: networks of asphalt radiating from traffic hubs or shopping malls, fast-food establishments with gaudy plastic fronts interspersed in billboard patterns with self-serve gas stations, drive-through banks, discount stores, warehouse groceries, coin-op laundries, convenience clinics, factory outlets, office areas dominated by aluminum and glass structures, and residential subdivisions featuring houses built on three floor plans or high-density condos for people who do not spend much time at home. The accrued message for the European was *transience.* For any objective observer, that impression of America is difficult to avoid as aesthetic judgment or historical overview, for in the United States during the span of time correlative with Kesey's life, the dominant fact of national history has been rapid change. The extent and frequency of changes—cultural, political, moral, social, techno-logical—occur with such rapidity that the American, as Marshall McLuhan once observed, often experiences his life as in a rearview mirror; he is moving too fast to see where he is going; he can see only where he has been, in a quickly diminishing vista that disappears before it can become either familiar or significant. The metaphor of the road is certainly appropriate for the peregrinations of Kesey and the Merry Pranksters, and a selected trip through the last five decades of American life will help to clarify the forces that formed Kesey's sensibility and contributed to the shaping of his fiction.

Although the depression that crippled America in the thirties did not affect Kesey directly as a child, it must certainly have influenced the values—the work ethic, the cherishing of family—that he inherited from his parents and grandparents. In the forties, however, Kesey, like other American children, had to live with World War II and all of its ramifications. The bombing of Pearl Harbor in 1941 served to unify Americans in their opposition to the worldwide threat of the madman anti-Semite and his kamikaze henchman, especially as the horrors of the Nazi concentration camps became public knowledge, but the dropping of the atomic bombs on Hiroshima and Nagasaki in 1945 made thoughtful Americans uneasy with their role as victors and liberators. The introduction of atomic power into the conflict effectively ended the war and catapulted America into the front rank of international superpowers, but it also established the irreversible possibility of global holocaust and thus left Americans, especially in the intellectual communities, with a pained conscience and a burdensome sense of responsibility for the future. That social conscience was tried further by widespread racial injustices in the country: the incarceration of Japanese-Americans in relocation camps, the treatment of Native Americans as second-class citizens by their confinement on reservations, and the legally sanctioned prejudices against black Americans. This last problem was mitigated after the war by, first, the breakdown of the racial barrier in professional baseball and by, second, President Truman's integration of the armed services late in the decade, two events that led to court-ordered racial integration in the mid-fifties. The mass of Americans, however, were not much affected by these matters of conscience as they enjoyed the fruits of victory and the financial gains of a postwar affluence.

America in the fifties looked very good to most Americans. Our industrial plant was undamaged by the war machine that had ravaged Europe, our land was untouched, and our quarter of a million war dead, though heartbreaking, seemed small in comparison, for example, to the almost twenty million fatalities suffered by Russia. Despite the anticommunist hysteria led by Senator Joe McCarthy and the House Committee on Un-American Activities, and the cold war that precipitated the Truman Doctrine, the general mood of the country was upbeat. President Eisenhower was an innocuous and popular president, the "silent generation" of college students quietly pursued vocational goals on campus, the economy was strong, and business was dominated by company men dedicated to conformity and the American way of profit. *Gentlemen Prefer Blondes* was among the most popular musicals of the period, and the number "I like Ike" was its showstopper. Rock-and-roll set America bopping, Elvis was king, television reared its spiky head, and the United States conducted a "police action" in Korea.

Critical or sobering voices there were, but they sounded from the periphery, not the center. From their coffeehouses on the West Coast, the beatniks expressed through their cool poetry and their studied passiveness a disdain for materialism and patriotism. David Riesman explored the consequences of conformity in *The Lonely Crowd* (1952). C. Wright Mill cautioned against the undemocratic operation of corporate power in *White Collar* (1951) and *The Power Elite* (1956). Vance Packard explored the subtle conditioning of advertising in *The Hidden Persuaders* (1957), while William H. Whyte's *The Organization Man* (1956) and John Kenneth Galbraith's *The Affluent Society* (1958) examined the nature, the excesses, and the dangers associated with a capitalistic controlling class and the creation of a mass society. Meanwhile, Alfred Kinsey issued two extensively documented reports—*Sexual Behavior of the American Male* (1948) and *Sexual Behavior of the American Female* (1953)—that challenged traditional notions of "normal" sexual activity and thus set the stage for a later sexual revolution. In 1954, the Supreme Court abolished racial segregation de jure by declaring "separate but equal facilities" unconstitutional. Courageous black leaders like Bayard Rustin, Roy Wilkins, and Martin Luther King, Jr., led civil rights protests to make the new ruling a social reality.

Whereas the fifties was mainly a time of quietude and conformity, the sixties, the period of Kesey's efflorescence, was a decade of turbulence and social unrest. The youthful optimism that was ushered in in 1961 with the inauguration of President Kennedy and his vision of a New Frontier was abruptly ended with his assassination only three years later. The Great Society that President Lyndon Johnson tried to institute was more a dream than an achievement, for his administration was beset by complicated problems at home and abroad. The technological ingenuity that had produced atomic power in the forties and televisions in the fifties developed space travel in the sixties, allowing the United States to put a manned spacecraft on the moon in July 1969, in what Neil Armstrong called a "giant step for mankind." The event was one of the few sources of national pride in the decade, for the American space program had to come from far behind to compete successfully with the Soviets' earlier achievements in the Sputnik launches. The patriotism generated by the space program, however, did not carry over to America's participation in the war in Vietnam. As the decade wore on and American involvement deepened, resistance to the unpopular and unwinnable war increased in most quarters of society.

Voices of dissent, protest, and critical analysis began to be heard everywhere, evidence of slipping confidence in American leadership, values, and models for happiness. As a result of the Berkeley Free Speech Movement (1964), the counterculture vision sponsored by hippies and communes, and a widespread political activism on college campuses, students began to insist on a voice in their own educations. Student-initiated "search" courses became commonly integrated into the standard curricula on the nation's campuses, with uneven results. Classes were often interrupted by political demonstrations for civil rights or protest marches against the war in Vietnam: "Hell no! We won't go!" or "Hey, Hey, LBJ. Have you nuked a Gook today?" Campus graffiti took on socialist colorations: "the people's elevator," "the people's water fountain." Young Americans for Freedom (YAF) debated Students for a Democratic Society (SDS). The Student Non-Violent Coordinating Committee (SNCC) tried with little success to balance incitement with restraint. The Congress of Racial Equality (CORE), the National Association for the Advancement of Colored People (NAACP), the Southern Christian Leadership Conference (SCLC), and the Black Panthers urged, with varying degrees of militancy, greater justice for blacks. Appearing in 1962, *One Flew Over the Cuckoo's Nest* captured at once the tumultuous unrest of the period, the idealism straining for direction, and the oppression many felt from strong but often unidentifiable outside forces. Civil rights activists made a march on Washington in 1963, where Dr. King delivered his famous "I Have a Dream" speech. The Gay Liberation Front urged tolerance for homosexuals. Women's Lib petitioned for equal opportunities and rewards for women, and the National Organization for Women (NOW) was founded in 1966. "Non-negotiable demands" and cries of "Right on!" proliferated. Although *Sometimes a Great Notion* (1964) stressed old-fashioned values and rugged individualism, it also touched on the restiveness of women in the characters of Myra and Viv and the disillusionment of educated American youth in the character of Lee. The center of Hank's Code-of-the West world held—but just barely. The sexual revolution was further advanced by the publication in 1966 of William H. Master's and Virginia E. Johnson's *Human Sexual Response*. The main sociological, ecological, and political texts for these various forms of agitation seemed to be Paul Goodman's *Growing Up Absurd* (1960), Rachel Carson's *Silent Spring* (1962), Betty Friedan's *The Feminine Mystique* (1963), Marshall McLuhan's *Understanding Media* (1964), Kenneth Kenniston's *The Young Radicals* (1968), Theodore Roszack's *The Making of a Counter-Culture* (1969), Herbert Marcuse's *An Essay on Liberation* (1969), and Charles A. Reich's *The Greening of America* (1970). The "flower children" of San Francisco and Woodstock, hipped on Zen and high on grass, preached peace and love while folk music (Bob Dylan, Joan Baez, Woody Guthrie) and rock (the Beatles, Jefferson Airplane, the Rolling Stones, the Grateful Dead) tried to soothe savage breasts, but the decade, with all its idealistic fervor, was still marred by destruction and death: Vietnam, the Charles Manson murders (1969), the assassinations of John Kennedy (1963), Malcolm X (1965), Martin Luther King, Jr. (1968), Robert Kennedy (1968), and what seemed an ineluctable conclusion to the confrontation between youth and the Establishment—the National Guard's killing of four students during a protest at Kent State University on 4 May 1970.

America entered the seventies, then, in a state of shock and increasing confusion over the extent and velocity of change in American life and values. While Kesey was gathering his emotional and psychological forces on the farm, the rest of the country was trying to get a handle on the new shape of things. In 1971, eighteen-year-olds got the vote. President Nixon was reelected in 1972 by sixty-seven percent of the popular vote, but by 1974 the Watergate Scandal forced him to resign a ruined man. In 1973, America withdrew its troops from Vietnam, leaving the troops and the nation settling for relief in the absence of victory or even progress in Southeast Asia. On the domestic front, there were some gains. The civil-rights movement succeeded in advancing the cause of justice for racial minorities (Aretha Franklin sang the message with a funky backbeat: R-E-S-P-E-C-T). The elderly, the sick, and the unemployed received a more humane share of the country's resources. State and federal agencies became more responsible about environmental protection. Per-capita income reached record levels. The scientific revolution accelerated. Solid-state calculators became shirt pocket items, and personal computers and video cassette recorders were almost as common in homes by the 1980s as food processors or trash compactors. Yet from the volatility of public affairs, open immorality, cavalier irresponsibility, and apparent indecisiveness in the highest office holders in the land, the temper of the populace was bewilderment, skepticism. Jimmy Carter defeated Gerald Ford for the presidency in 1976, but he lost in turn to Ronald Reagan in 1980 largely as a consequence of the perception, resulting from the hostage affair in Iran, that America had become impotent and directionless in national purpose and international relations.

Personal stresses matched public ones during the 1970s. Under the influence of the times and the admonitions of free-wheeling books like Abbie Hoffman's *Revolution for the Hell of It* (1968) and Jerry

Rubin's *Do It* (1970), hippies had to make room for "yippies," who were programmed to "do their own thing," a solipsistic impulse that led Tom Wolfe in "The Me Decade and the Third Great Awakening" (1976) to characterize those entering adulthood in the seventies as the self-indulgent, hedonistic "me" generation. Disco music, Muzak with a beat, spawned discotheques where urban escapists could gyrate in parallel patterns without touching. Sexual mores continued to evolve rapidly, as evinced in Kate Millett's *Sexual Politics* (1970), Germaine Greer's *The Female Eunuch* (1971), Hugh Hefner's *Playboy* philosophy, widely available pornography, and relaxed restraints on both network and cable television. Two key works for the period were Alvin Toffler's *Future Shock* (1970) and Vance Packard's *A Nation of Strangers* (1972), both charting the present and possible effects of overwhelming changes: a growing nomadic population, the dissolution of families, opportunistic job-changing, curtailed and discontinuous personal relationships, reduced civic consciousness and social responsibility, physical neglect of public facilities, and self-destructive psychological anxieties. Shaky detente with Russia and the growing fear of imminent nuclear genocide exacerbated the search for identity and stability in an uneasy decade.

The election of Ronald Reagan in 1980 and his reelection in 1984 set the stamp of conservatism on America in the eighties. His presidency resulted in part from a rising right-wing influence that included these factions: a coalition of neoconservative eastern intellectuals; the Moral Majority dominated by fundamentalist television ministers and their followers; Nixon's "Silent Majority"; and a loosely organized group of individuals and business-oriented activists called the New Right. Reagan also benefited, however, from a nostalgic yearning in the populace at large for a return to the model of an earlier and less complicated nation. Part of the nostalgia resulted from fatigue following years of political upheaval, part from relief that America had survived a number of real crises, and part from the simple fact that the activists of the sixties and seventies were now older and more concerned with their own families and vocations than with political ideology. Moreover, some genuine gains had been made. Despite its costs in lives and money, and despite the frustrating terms of withdrawal, the undeclared war in Vietnam was over. However humiliating the spectacle to the national ego, the hostages held by Iran had been returned home safely despite a bungled rescue attempt. Although Reagan won the 1984 election, Geraldine Ferraro was the Democratic nominee for vice president, the first woman to be nominated by a major political party for the second highest office in the federal government. Women became increasingly prominent as mayors, judges, congresswomen, and corporate executives, and Sandra Day O'Connor sat as a justice on the Supreme Court. Minorities, too, gained greater access to the professions, to government, and to business. Philadelphia, Chicago, and Atlanta elected black mayors. Above all, business was booming. "Careerism" shaped the thinking of the "yuppies" (young urban professionals) and the "dinks" (double income, no kids), and everyone in the business community read with renewed interest the latest investment advice in magazines such as *Fortune, Forbes,* and *Money.* Consumers pored over the comparative quality of a plethora of products reviewed in *Consumer Reports.* The stock market set one record after another for volume of trading, and the Dow average soared to an all-time high. Lee Iacocca moved from Ford to the failing Chrysler Corporation and, with the aid of some government subsidy, miraculously restored it to financial health. His account of his life, *Iacocca* (1984), became a best-seller, and Iacocca was seen as the epitome of the courageous and resourceful leader and thus a potential candidate for the presidency of the United States. *Time*'s Man of the Year for 1982 was not a man at all, however, but the computer. Known as the "teflon" president because voters seemed to ignore or forgive his mistakes—like the terrorist killing of 241 Marines in Beruit—Reagan presided benignly over the nation's apparent prosperity, but threatening clouds hovered over the American landscape.

Kesey's major publication in the eighties was *The Demon Box* (1986), in which the novelist had to contend in a kind of exorcism with the misjudgments and excesses of his past. Likewise, America in the eighties was forced to confront the consequences of its excesses and errors, and by 1987—a year of scandal—these were monumental. The intellectual and attitudinal shortcomings of American students and the pedagogical and philosophical flaws of the institutions trying to educate them were scrutinized in two influential academic books in 1987: Allan Bloom's *The Closing of the American Mind: How Higher Education Has Failed Democracy and Impoverished the Souls of Today's Students* and E. D. Hirsch, Jr.'s *Cultural Literacy: What Every American Needs to Know.* The national debt rose to about $300 billion annually, and neither Congress nor the president had the courage to propose a balanced budget. Although business activity in America was intense, American hegemony in international trade had been a thing of the past. Germany and Japan clobbered the United States in production, marketing, quality control, and exporting. The dollar fell regularly against the mark and the yen. An oil glut brought the American oil industry to its knees, and formerly oil-rich states like Texas suffered unprecedented unemployment, mortgage foreclosures, bank failures, and demoralization. Chrysler's upward surge early in the decade was slowed by a discovery of widespread odometer tampering and other misbehavior by many of its dealers and possibly some of its corporate executives. Wall Street was stricken by startling cases of insider trading.

Two television evangelists fell from grace: Jim Bakker was defrocked as the fundamentalist pastor of the multimillion-dollar PTL ministry for his sexual transgressions and financial sleight-of-hand, and Jimmy Swaggart was suspended from the Assembly of God ministry of his comparably rich television empire for pornographic activity with a prostitute. Lawsuits amounting to $1.3 billion were filed in twenty-three states against various Catholic priests for alleged sexual abuse of children, especially of altar boys. Former Colorado Governor Gary Hart was forced to abandon his presidential aspirations—temporarily at least—because of public disclosure early in his campaign of his sexual indiscretions. U.S. Marines were sent home from the American Embassy in Moscow and placed under criminal investigation for allegedly trading national security secrets for sex with Russian women.

In what may prove the scandal of the eighties, Marine Lt. Colonel Oliver North confessed under congressional investigation to illegal weapons sales to Iran and connected illegal military support operations in South America that implicated at least retired Rear Admiral John M. Poindexter, CIA Director William J. Casey, Secretary of State George P. Shultz, Assistant Secretary of State Elliott Abrams, Vice Admiral Arthur Moreau, National Security Advisor Robert McFarlane, Vice President George Bush, and President Reagan himself.

Although women continued to make progress toward equality with men in the marketplace, the Equal Rights Amendment remained unratified since it was defeated in Congress in 1982. Surrounded by corruption and confusion, the youth of America in great numbers seemed to find the objective correlatives for their feelings in the fractious, libidinous, and indiscriminately violent music of MTV fare in groups like Twisted Sister, Heavy Metal, Poison, and Motley Crüe. Crime rates rose, and the nation's prisons groaned from overcrowding. The sexual revolution was stalled by the appearance of AIDS and herpes, sexually related diseases for which there was no cure and, in the case of the former, no hope. AIDS had claimed thousands of lives in the early eighties, but by mid-decade more attention was focused on the disease when its victims included actor Rock Hudson, pianist Liberace, and choreographer/director Michael Bennett. In their sexual report for the eighties, William Masters and Virginia Johnson (with Robert Kolodny) warned in *Crisis: Heterosexual Behavior in the Age of AIDS* (1988) that the AIDS virus "will now begin to escalate at a frightening pace."

America in the eighties seemed to be a rabid wolf consuming its own entrails. No wonder, then, that as the decade wound down, Kesey turned from the chaos of the contemporary scene to focus his imagination on the lives of cowboys in Oregon in 1911 and on the pristine wildness of Alaska as America's last frontier, where, perhaps, the Code of the West still had some meaning.

2

THE IMPORTANCE OF THE WORK

One Flew Over the Cuckoo's Nest invites assessment on many grounds—mimetic, formal, psychological, mythical, among others—and these dimensions of the work will come under examination in due course. The central importance of the novel as a classic text, though, is mainly twofold: 1) it embodies in modern form a long-standing tension in American life and literature between the individual and society and between optimism and pessimism, and 2) it affirms heroism in the face of universal absurdity, alienation, and overwhelmingly destructive forces. A glance at some older American writers and a brief look at three recent books of literary criticism will provide the necessary framework for understanding the remarkable resonance that the novel has struck in its many readers past and present.

The placement of McMurphy in the mental ward between the oppressive forces of The Combine and Big Nurse on one side and the oppressed ranks of the individual inmates on the other points up the historical polarity in America between the many and the one, between mass society and its "norms" of conformity and the individual and his impulse to freedom, between pessimism about human weakness and optimism about human strength. The conflict is evident in earlier

American literature in Natty Bumppo's trekking ever westward to escape the encroachments of civilization on his individual liberty, or later in Huck Finn's "lighting out for the territory" for the same reason. A similar polarity divided the eighteenth century between the Calvinistic pessimism and sternly rigid morality of Jonathan Edwards and the cheerful deistic optimism of the pragmatically flexible Benjamin Franklin. Although Emerson in the nineteenth century lived in the community and was for a while its minister, his message, in "Self-Reliance" for example, was "Society everywhere is in conspiracy against the manhood of every one of its members," and "Whoso would be a man, must be a nonconformist." In "Civil Disobedience," Thoreau played a variation on the same theme. If the law, he said, is "of such a nature that it requires you to be the agent of injustice to another, then, I say, break the law." Whitman expressed the matter poetically. In one of the "Inscriptions" to *Song of Myself,* he intoned, "One's-self I sing, a simple separate person, / Yet utter the word Democratic, the word En-Masse." For Hawthorne, the conflict was a moral one. However admirable the personal qualities of Hester Prynne, she was a rebel, and society, for the sake of moral order, had to protect itself against such rebellions. In "The Maypole of Merry Mount," Hawthorne wrote, "Jollity and gloom were contending for an empire," a comment, as he knew, that characterized an American conflict far beyond the confrontation of the Puritan Endicott with the hedonists at Merry Mount. The conflict between Big Nurse and McMurphy, then, carries the weight of American literary history. She is the tyrannical puppet of the societal forces of conformity. He is the individual free spirit running (at many revolutions per minute) on joie de vivre, resisting rules, and seeking life's pleasures where he can find them.

Tony Tanner's *City of Words* and Josephine Hendin's *Vulnerable People* have explored the increasingly complex nature of these polarities as they are reflected in contemporary American fiction. For Tanner, "there is an abiding dream in American literature that an unpatterned, unconditioned life is possible, in which your movements and stillnesses, choices and repudiations are all your own; and there is also an abiding American dread that someone else is patterning your life, that there are all sorts of invisible plots afoot to rob you of your autonomy of thought and action, that conditioning is ubiquitous."[1] For Hendin, Tanner's dread-versus-dream pattern assumes the form of a search to reduce personal vulnerability to the various threats of modern life. It is a search for "shock-resistant lives," and in American fiction the search alternates between two extremes: "One is holistic, stressing the virtues of management, wholeness, reason. The other is anarchic, stressing the mystical values of self-effacement and disintegration. . . . Holistic and anarchic fiction each explode the traditional concerns of the novel in directions which reflect the course of American life."[2] Kesey's novel skillfully depicts the dread and the anarchic impulses. The conspiracy of social conditioning is the Combine; Big Nurse patterns the lives of the inmates. The anarchic impulse to disintegration is evident in the voluntary commitment of the men to the hospital's confinement, in Bromden's withdrawal into the fog, in Cheswick's and Bibbit's suicides. The black humor in the novel, which attempts through caricature to buffer pain with laughter, is the generic shape of the anarchic impulse. But the greatness of *One Flew Over the Cuckoo's Nest* is its transcendence of the negative to affirm the positive, the triumph of the dream over the dread, and that affirmation requires a hero.

"McMurphy," Kesey has revealed, "was fictional, inspired by the tragic longing of real men I worked with on the ward [the psychiatric ward of the Menlo Park VA hospital]."[3] That is, Kesey as humane novelist created his heroic fictive protagonist from the real needs of actual men debilitated by the formidable strengths of the external world and by their own frailties. The disparity between human aspirations and the level of actual achievements allowed by a recalcitrant reality has come to be known existentially as the "absurd." The confrontation with the absurd can lead to despair and disintegration, as it did with Cheswick and Bibbit, the triumph of the dread over the dream. Suicide, Albert Camus observed in *The Myth of Sisyphus*, becomes the first philosophical question after the encounter with the absurd. The absurd, however, can inspire heroic resistance and spiritual transcendence. David Galloway has explained the process: ". . . There is a recognizable and highly consequential tradition in Western literature whereby the absurd—as defined by Albert Camus—

becomes a way of affirming the resources of the human spirit, of exalting sacrifice and suffering, of ennobling the man capable of sustaining the vital opposition between intention and reality."[4] The triumph of Sisyphus over his rock is a metaphor for the modern hero's victory over his absurd situation and hostile environment. McMurphy's defiance and martyrdom and Bromden's discipleship are squarely in that tradition.

Here lies the essential power of *One Flew Over the Cuckoo's Nest*. The growth of McMurphy from con man to hero to savior is a paradigm of the successful struggle of the individual against at once an oppressive society, his own human weaknesses, and cosmic indifference to his wishes and welfare. That McMurphy is finally willing to sacrifice his life to restore life to others is a testament to values more important than mere survival—freedom, dignity, pride, love, courage—and thus an imposition of human significance on the absurd. Readers believe in McMurphy's growth because it has its living counterpart in Chief Bromden, who tells the story and whose intimate first-person narration enables the readers to experience with him his transformation under McMurphy's salvific influence from sickness to health, from weakness to strength, from cowardice to heroism. The message of *Cuckoo's Nest* is that something can be done about absurdity. The liberation of Bromden at the end stands for the liberation of Everyman from the clutches of intimidation, fear, and bad faith. Such optimism is rare in a sea of nay-sayers, but it has a long tradition in the bipolar canon of American literature, and Kesey earns his positive vision by his unflinching documentation of the forces aligned against affirmation and heroism in the modern world.

3

CRITICAL RECEPTION

With the book now in its sixty-eighth printing and with seven million copies in circulation, *Cuckoo's Nest* has engaged a great many readers for over a quarter of a century and engendered a range of responses broad enough and serious enough to justify the classification of the book as a modern classic. When it appeared in 1962, it seemed to carry a special message for every segment of society. Many young people found reinforcement in the novel for their own resentment of flinty, misguided authority and for their open pursuit of a spontaneous, sensual life. Adults received confirmation of their own uneasy fears that government and technology had assumed monstrous lives of their own alien to the commonweal, and that morality and law had been institutionalized beyond the reach of common sense and justice. The old and the incapacitated felt that their pervasive sense of victimization had been given a local habitat and a name and that their cause had discovered a champion. People everywhere seemed uplifted by McMurphy's compassion and willingness to sacrifice his life so that others might live and by Bromden's Phoenix-like regeneration. On the negative side, some readers complained that the novel was marred by an overreliance on caricature, contrivance, or simplistic vision, by an in-

024708

sensitive or misogynistic treatment of women, by nihilistic or anti-intellectual biases, or by blatant racism. These views and others have found their formal expression in reviews, articles, and books spread over the last twenty-four years.

The reviews of Kesey's first novel were mainly positive and enthusiastic, but some were mixed, and a few were negative. A sampling shows the spread. In an enthusiastic review in the *Chicago Sunday Tribune Magazine of Books* (4 February 1962), R. A. Jelliffe emphasized the mixture of realism and myth in what he called a "bi-tonal technique of terrible realism in conjunction with a profound and searching parable of government and the governed." Rose Feld observed in the *New York Herald Tribune Book Review* (25 February 1962) that "undoubtedly there will be controversy over some material in Ken Kesey's novel but there can be none about his talent." In the *New York Times Book Review* (4 February 1962), Martin Levin called the novel "a glittering parable of good and evil." In London, the *Times Literary Supplement* (3 May 1963) said that "first and foremost here is an exact work of fiction, always a little preposterous, never suspiciously biographic, with a spare but flowing style and an imagery that matches the fear of pills, shock therapy and starched white uniforms." *Time* (16 February 1962) admired Kesey's power and humor and characterized his book as "a strong, warm story about the nature of human good and evil, despite the macabre setting." In *Library Journal* (1 February 1962), George Adelman affirmed "this is the best novel I have read for a long time."

Novelist and critic William Peden, writing in the *Saturday Review* (14 April 1962), enthusiastically welcomed a new talent to the guild: "His storytelling is so effective, his style so impetuous, his grasp of characters so certain that the reader is swept along in McMurphy's boisterous wake. . . . Mr. Kesey, in short, has created a world that is convincing, alive, and glowing within its own boundaries and in terms of his own ground rules." In a similar vein ran most of the endorsements of Kesey's work.

In some other reviews, however, commentary ranged from mild reservations about the novel to vehement denunciation. Although W.

J. Smith characterized Kesey as "a rough diamond," he argued that the book lacked direction and that much of the "real horror and significance" was vitiated by "some quite misplaced slapstick" (*Commonweal*, 16 March 1962). Irving Malin wrote in *Critique* (vol. 5, 1962) that Kesey's work belonged to a "new American Gothic" that disrupts rational worldviews to present "violent juxtapositions, distorted vision, even prophecy without becoming completely private." Although *Cuckoo's Nest* was a "stylistically brilliant first novel," said Malin, he felt Kesey did not probe deeply enough into the philosophical issues raised in the book, that Kesey was a "poet, not a philosopher." The reviewer of *Kirkus* (1 December 1961) found the book an "enthralling, brilliantly tempered novel" but felt it was limited in scope as "a ward and *not* a microcosm" and that it was likely to be taken "too seriously." The *New Yorker* (21 April 1962) gave the book short shrift, calling it "an almost novel, made up largely of symbols and a rapid shuffle of black-and-white vignettes" and describing its style as "pastepot colloquial." Almost ten years after the novel had been adapted as a play, Marcia L. Falk expressed her outrage at the vision she perceived in both forms: the novel/play "never once challenges the completely inhuman sexist structure of society, nor does it make any attempt to overthrow sexist or racist stereotypes. The only blacks in the play are stupid and malicious hospital orderlies. And the only right-on women in the play are mindless whores." According to Falk, "Nurse Ratched is a woman because Ken Kesey hates and fears women. And apparently Dale Wasserman along with everyone else who helped adapt Kesey's novel . . . are so thoroughly conditioned by the basic sexist assumptions of our society that they never even noticed, or cared to question, the psychic disease out of which the book's vision was born" (*New York Times*, 5 December 1971, letter to the editor).

The articles on *Cuckoo's Nest* that appeared in professional journals usually lacked the emotional charge of the Falk opinion, as one would expect, but as they ranged from thematic to generic to technical matters, they had the cumulative effect of revealing the remarkable scope of a novel that appeared initially to be almost allegorical in its simplicity of structure and theme despite its density of texture. That scope, for instance, moved Lehigh University to hold a symposium in the late 1970s on the nature and ramifications of Kesey's novel. The proceedings of the symposium were published in a double issue of *Lex et Scientia* (the International Journal of Law and Science). In his introductory remarks to the volume, John W. Hunt accented the diversity of the novel:

> The emergence of the novel in play and movie forms is only one evidence of how Kesey's original work has increasingly become a novel which must be reckoned with. The evolving hero, the fool as mentor, the psychopathic savior, the cosmic Christ, the Grail Knight, the comic strip Lone Ranger, attitudes toward sex, the fear of women, abdication of masculinity, the politics of laughter, mechanistic and totemistic symbolization—these phrases or variations upon them, reading like a list of special topics courses offered at an avant-garde liberals arts college, can be found in the titles given in the bibliography in this symposium collection.[5]

The symposium collection, edited by Hunt and Peter Beidler, contained seventeen articles and a bibliography. A brief examination of some of these items and of selected articles from other journals will provide useful expansion of the subject areas listed above and thus specify the further dimensions of Kesey's novel.

In the *Lex et Scientia* volume, Leslie Horst took Kesey to task for offering a liberation to the inmates based on a narrow traditional definition of sex roles, including a truncated concept of masculinity ("Bitches, Twitches, and Eunuchs: Sex-Role Failure and Caricature"). Peter G. Beidler focused on Bromden, tracing his literary heritage from such figures as Chingachgook, the noble Indian hero of Cooper's *Last of the Mohigans* (1826), and Tonto and showing how Kesey reverses our expectations by transforming "mere natural man, . . . an innocent pupil to be educated by the Great White Father," into a fully integrated man who is saved from the Combine ("Ken Kesey's Indian Narrator: A Sweeping Stereotype?"). Hunt argued that Bromden functions in the novel to validate the fictive vision, that the "normative in the novel is the truth which the story . . . yields for Bromden" ("Flying the Cuckoo's Nest: Kesey's Narrator as Norm"). Addison C. Bross took the opposite view. For him, the novel "does not present us with a convincingly imagined world, but instead bases its appeal on a certain popular ideology . . . that a repressive Establishment is in command of our world" ("Art and Ideology: Kesey's Approach to Fiction"). Edward J. Gallagher grounded his reading of the novel on recurrent themes in science fiction and concluded that *Cuckoo's Nest* is about men turning into machines, about excessive control and dehumanization in a secular, technological society ("From Folded Hands to Clenched Fists: Kesey and Science Fiction"). Roger C. Loeb, on the other hand, felt that Kesey had done the medical profession a disservice with his mechanistic depiction of mental hospitals and mental health professionals ("Machines, Mops, and Medicaments: Therapy in the Cuckoo's Nest"). Jack DeBellis examined Kesey's characters and themes in the context of older American literature ("Alone No More: Dualism in American Literary Thought"), and Joan Bischoff placed Kesey in alignment with the bleak, entropic vision of more recent black humor writers ("Everything Running Down: Ken Kesey's Vision of Imminent Entropy"). Annette Benert perceived the essential power of the novel in its depiction of human triumph not over external forces but over internal ones with ancient roots ("The Forces of Fear: Kesey's Anatomy of Insanity"):

> The Novel continues to compel an audience because it makes deep connections to several important strands of American psychic life— fear of women, fear of the machine, and glorification of the hero who conquers both. The Terrible Mother of ancient mythology reappears as a frozen and fearsome Big Nurse, in imagery as transparent as the glass cage surrounding her. The Devouring Dragon has become the dynamo, the locomotive, the mad computer, the Combine—an all-powerful electronic presence permeating the souls of men. Into this nightmare world comes the Savior, all red hair, libido, and cowboy bravado, whose reluctant heroism earns him an electronic crucifixion.(22)

The interdisciplinary nature of the essays in this volume testifies to the far-reaching significance of Kesey's vision and his fictive forms, in a novel that has what Hunt called in his introduction "a vital staying power, a continuing relevance to our changing society."

Articles elsewhere work some of the same soil as well as cultivate adjoining fields. According to Terence Martin, Big Nurse has her antecedent in Orwell's Big Brother, and the basic conflict in the novel occurs in a giant-screen confrontation between a misguided matriarchy and a resistant patriarchy: "As the contours of the narrative take form, the bigger-than-life McMurphy and the bigger-than-life Miss Ratched come to be opposed in every way. He is the stud, she the ball-cutter; he is the brawler, she the manufacturer of docility; he is the gambler, she the representative of the house—where chance has no meaning."[6] Where Martin sees this caricature-conflict as successful, Robert Forrey sees it as a sexist sham: "*One Flew Over the Cuckoo's Nest* was written from the point of view that man's problems are caused by woman who refuses to allow him to play the domineering role which nature intended him to play. The premise of the novel is that women ensnare, emasculate, and, in some cases, crucify men."[7] Terry Sherwood explains that Kesey comes to his caricatures by way of popular culture—the folk song, the western movie, the comic strip: "For Kesey, the heavenly Christ and the supernatural comic book hero stand on common mythic ground as images of human potential. McMurphy's self-regarding and independent pursuit of physical pleasure, inspirited by defiant laughter and gambler's unconcern for security, make him superior to other men and free him from society; his power of miracle is transmitting his traits to others. . . . He has the superhero's efficacious physical power but, like Christ, the magnitude of his threat to society forces his crucifixion."[8] McMurphy's messianic function, says John Wilson Foster, is mythically based on the necessary death of the hero: "Kesey uses his Christ-symbolism to suggest that McMurphy is a man of Christly motives whose 'crucifixion' redeems the sinners around him."[9] For William J. Handy, however, McMurphy's and Bromden's heroism and Kesey's vision and forms are derived not so much from mythic or biblical sources as from modern existentialism: "It is McMurphy, an alien to every world he inhabits, up against the absurd mechanism of the Combine, who makes the decision to sacrifice his own existence in order to support the existences of the inmates of the mental ward—a response, Kesey writes, to 'orders beamed at him from forty masters.'"[10] The debate over the meanings and merits of the novel continues steadily in the pages of literary journals, extending Kesey's reputation from the street to the halls of ivy.

Among the many scholarly books that include sections on Kesey, at least four should be mentioned here to indicate the variety of critical perspectives. In *The Return of the Vanishing American* (1968), Leslie Fiedler suggests that the new frontier is not the Old West, but the New West, which he defines as experimentation with drugs initially and transcendence into madness finally. The old savage was the red man; the new savage is the black man. Kesey's personal life and his use of McMurphy and Bromden in a drug-controlled madhouse are models of the new exploration, and, says Fiedler, McMurphy and Bromden are linked in the American canon to older pairings: Natty Bumppo/ Chingachgook, Ishmael/Queequeg, Huck/Jim, Lone Ranger/Tonto. For Raymond M. Olderman, *Cuckoo's Nest* is a modern retelling of the Grail legend in "waste land" imagery. McMurphy is the Grail Knight who enters the waste land to heal the wounded Fisher King (Bromden) by defeating the enchantress Madame Sosostris (Big Nurse) to restore the true meanings of the magic words *Give, Sympathize,* and *Control,* which Big Nurse has corrupted and exploited (*Beyond the Waste Land: The American Novel in the Sixties,* 1972). Ronald Wallace takes a generic approach to the novel. In *The Last Laugh: Form and Affirmation in the Contemporary American Comic Novel* (1979), he classifies the novel as comedy, not a romance, using the Bergsonian theory of comic incongruity, which assumes the form of role reversals in *Cuckoo's Nest*: people as machines (Big Nurse, the Combine), slaves as masters (the aides), women as men (Big Nurse), men as women (Harding, Billy, Bromden's father). McMurphy is the *eiron* (the witty self-deprecator) who must defeat the *alazon* (the imposter and self-deceived fool) and give the life of laughter to the surviving Chief.[11] Jack Hicks groups Kesey with Marge Piercy and Richard Brautigan as "countercultural" writers who are more engaged by the nature of human consciousness than by the chaos of human events (*In the Singer's Temple: Prose Fictions of Barthelme, Gaines, Brautigan, Piercy, Kesey, and Kosinski*, 1981).

In addition to the unpublished but oft-quoted dissertation by Ronald G. Billingsley at Oregon (1971), there have been at least eleven other doctoral dissertations on Kesey and his work and, in recent years, four monographs, all attempting to understand the writer and his fiction in the context of his times. The dissertations are beyond the scope of this discussion, but a brief look at the general focus of the monographs is certainly appropriate here. In his pamphlet in the Western Writers Series, Bruce Carnes asserts that in *Cuckoo's Nest* "Kesey presents a world of moral extremes in which the Enemy and the Hero are clearly distinguishable; he shows us a society which, though it has not yet succeeded in stifling every individual, nevertheless controls most aspects of human behavior. In that world heroism, though very difficult, is both necessary and possible and can lead to the salvation of society. . . . Kesey's first book shows us that the American dream is valid: one can be what he wants to be and can do what he wants to do."[12] Barry Leeds employs close critical analysis of the techniques of symbolism, structure, and characterization in *Cuckoo's Nest* and accounts for the continuing "relevance" of the issues it explores: "The questioning of a monolithic bureaucratic order, the rejection of stereotyped sexual roles, the simultaneous awareness that healthy sexuality and a clear sense of sexual identity are prerequisite for human emotional survival, the recognition and rejection of hypocrisy, the devotion to the expression of individual identity."[13] For M. Gilbert Porter, Kesey is a synecdochist in *Cuckoo's Nest,* and Bromden is both his spokesman and a test case for the salvific powers of courage and love: "Thus Kesey uses motifs of significant parts: laughs, hands, faces. Each motif is fully developed and tightly integrated into the novel's central design, and Bromden as narrator is the most important device in Kesey's use of synecdoche. The most broken of all the fragmented lives in the story, Bromden's is the most dramatically restored at the end. His developing mental health is a paradigm writ large for the similar development of the others."[14] Stephen L. Tanner provides a broad interpretive spectrum from other critics and then offers his own reading in terms of a formal division "into four parts of cycles of action that are approximately parallel in structure. At the beginning of each cycle the Big Nurse is either ascendant or biding her time incubating a new strategy of attack, and at the end McMurphy or what he represents is ascendant. There is progression in the movement from cycle to cycle, however, for despite setbacks, McMurphy by the end of each part has brought Bromden closer to the freedom from fear that constitutes his salvation."[15] That other critics will find still other ore to mine from this rich novel is both inevitable and desirable; in the intellectual exchanges between writer and reader, between reader and critic, and between students and teachers, everyone is enriched, the enterprise of literature is preserved, and general human understanding is advanced.

Kesey's novel will continue to generate controversy and invite further analysis, for it is a book of basic conflicts and almost infinitely multiplying cultural connotations. Kesey himself, however, has indicated that he sees the novel in a less complicated way than many of his critics. Peter Whitmer reported in the *Saturday Review* that Kesey thinks of *Cuckoo's Nest* as "a Christian allegory that deals with good and evil," in which "McMurphy is the Christian character, the powerful Western Hero, willing to put his life on the line for the downtrodden. The evil is a sickness in the American consciousness that Kesey symbolizes by the 'combine.' The evil is not the government, not the cops, and certainly not Big Nurse."[16] The attempts to identify the "evil," the "sickness in the American consciousness," to trace its sources, and to explore its contexts, forms, and ramifications have led the critics of the novel—apologists and detractors—to discover that *Cuckoo's Nest* goes well beyond simple allegory. What they discover is that Kesey wrought deeper than he knew. Such resonance is the mark of fine art. It is what keeps readers and explicators returning to the novel again and again.

A Reading

American literature in the sixties was shaped in large measure by its reactions to social, technological, and ethical changes and to altered modes of apprehending reality. Often the literary responses were as extreme as the changes that provoked them. Malcolm Bradbury has explored the issue as it is reflected in the American novel: "American fiction at the beginning of the Sixties was enlarging its themes and looking historically outward; it was also reappraising the forces loose in the world, and the individual's power to face them. The history novelists now explored was somehow beyond individual existence and the measure of reason; it was a history of distorting power plays, large conspiratorial structures, huge technological systems, apocalyptic threats to survival."[17] The impotent and increasingly insignificant individual in conflict with the irrational, the absurd, or some "large conspirational structure" certainly describes the deployment of forces in *Cuckoo's Nest* as well as a common pattern in other novels of the decade. Two novels whose dates of publication form bookends to *Cuckoo's Nest* provide representative and useful contrasts.

In *Catch-22* (1961), Joseph Heller employs war as his microcosm of madness, in contrast to Kesey's microcosmic mental ward, and Captain Yosarian, the combat airman, as his protagonist. The absolute absurdity of war, the horror of death, the irrationality of "Catch-22" (the military "double-gotcha" that perpetuates combat by exploiting human life through official policy) drive Yosarian to go AWOL. At the end, he makes a separate peace by fleeing to neutral Sweden. Heller's answer to absurdity is to try to escape from it. In Thomas Pynchon's *V* (1963), absurdity takes the form of an intellectual quest to discover the meaning of the mysterious symbol "V." Herbert Stencil, the protagonist, conducts the search all over the world and in a vast array of official documents. He discovers that "V" means so many things that it finally means nothing unequivocally, that intelligence has led him to discover that intelligence is ultimately useless in a totally irrational and entropic world. Benny Profane, the leader of the Whole Sick Crew, has come to the same conclusion yo-yoing in the streets; from his experiences, he reveals, he has "not learned a goddamn thing." His conclusions stands as a kind of caption to Stencil's theoretical quest and his own practical one and seems to sum up as well Pynchon's assessment of the hopeless plight of the rational in the world against the irrational. Both of these novels play mainly and successfully for laughs in the postmodernist traditions of black humor or fabulation, but the vision underlying the humor is intended seriously, and the bleakness of that vision is unsettling to those who come to literature for inspiration and direction. These novels reflect a constant tongue-in-cheek attitude of the authors toward the relation between their fiction and reality.

Kesey's novel also plays for laughs and employs many of the techniques of fabulation and certainly documents an equivalent level of absurdity in the world. The major difference, though, is that Kesey believes fiction is a valid form of knowledge about human reality, and he is more sanguine in *Cuckoo's Nest* about the resources of the individual against external forces, more hopeful about the chances for growth in character and change in society, equally aware of but less intimidated by the powers of various collective forces in the external world. He seems to share a strong conviction with Bromden: "Maybe the Combine wasn't all-powerful."[18] The message of the novel is that something can be done about absurdity whether it is encountered in the human spirit or in human institutions.

The power of *Cuckoo's Nest* inheres in part, then, in Kesey's positive tone that stubbornly persists against the almost overwhelming evidence for negation in the book and in the world it depicts. But that novelistic power derives entirely from Kesey's careful craftsmanship. Although he may use along the way some of the postmodern techniques, Kesey is fundamentally an old-fashioned literary artist working with traditional themes and the basic elements of fiction—story, plot, character, symbol—and whatever innovative devices he employs are always skillfully integrated into conventional forms that he has somehow made anew and thus transformed into fiction that is uniquely his own. The reading that follows examines setting, plot, characterization, symbolism, and point of view in *Cuckoo's Nest* in a discovery of meaning through form. The organic unity of this novel is particularly rewarding to such an approach.

4

SETTING

As a Northwesterner and a man who lives close to the soil, Kesey is deeply involved with his surroundings and keenly aware of the relation of his fiction to the various configurations of the social and natural environments that inspire his writing. Like other regional writers, he is sensitive to the importance of place in the conditioning of sensibilities, the shaping of attitudes, and the formation of values. Eudora Welty states the matter well:

> Like a good many other writers, I am touched off by place. The place where I am and the place I know, and other places that familiarity with and love for my own make strange and lovely and enlightening to look into, are what set me to writing my stories. To such writers I suppose place opens a door in the mind, either spontaneously or through beating it down, attrition. The impression of place as revealing something is an indelible one—which of course is not to say it isn't highly personal and very likely distorted. The imagination further and further informs and populates the impression according to present mood, intensification of feeling, beat of memory, accretion of idea, and by the blessing of being located—contained—a story so charged is now capable of being written.[19]

The experiences that opened the creative doors for Kesey occurred in California in the seminar rooms at Palo Alto, in parties and rap sessions on Perry Lane, and in hospital wards in Menlo Park, but in the transmutation of experience into art, Kesey relocated his world in Oregon, where familiar landmarks provided some stabilizing boundaries for a microcosm psychically out of kilter. Kesey's California experiences suggested a mental ward, but his roots in the Oregon outdoors suggested reality. The choice of a Columbia Gorge half-breed for narrator gave Kesey some aesthetic distance from his work yet provided the intensity of feeling, the distortion, and the erratic blend of memory and observation necessary to reveal through first-person narration the startling relations between Inside and Outside from one who has been fully demoralized in both settings. Bromden enters the ward to escape the world, the Combine, then enters his self-induced fog to escape the ward. Kesey's strategy is to use McMurphy to reverse Bromden's movement through the settings of the novel.

THE INSIDE

As Bromden describes it, the inside of the cuckoo's nest is a place of nightmarish order and brain-deadening routine. The walls of the hospital are immaculate white, and they hum day and night with mysterious machinery. From the spotless glass-enclosed Nurses' Station in the day room, Big Nurse operates the controls and directs the activities that propel the inmates through their monotonous days, their gray faces and convalescent greens in the fluorescent lights forming a ghostly contrast with the white walls. Every day the same musical tape plays as a mindless background to the activities in the ward. With rare exception, each day is the same: wake-up at six-thirty, shave at six-forty-five, breakfast at seven, division of inmates in the day room at seven-thirty, cards, puzzles, and magazines at eight, special assignments on Order Daily cards to Physical Therapy, Occupational Therapy, Electro-Shock Therapy, or Therapeutic Community Meeting for the rest of the morning, lunch at noon, then back to the day room and another identical round of activities. Bromden thinks that Big Nurse controls the passage of time with a dial in the Nurses' Station, speeding it up during infrequent enjoyable periods, dragging it out incessantly during the typical dull periods, and sometimes stopping it altogether and encasing it in plastic. The ward appears superficially to be a place of order and purposeful activity. In fact, it is a grotesque world of tortured individuals "like puppets, mechanical puppets in one of those Punch and Judy acts where it's supposed to be funny to see the puppet beat up by the Devil and swallowed headfirst by a smiling alligator . . ."(37).

The puppets in the ward are classified as Acutes or Chronics. Acutes are sick but salvageable. Chronics, subclassified as Walkers, Wheelers, and Vegetables, are beyond reclamation. All of those in the inside are misfits—the weak, the different, the slow, the fearful—who could not cope with the outside. "The ward," says Bromden, "is a factory for the Combine. It's for fixing mistakes made in the neighborhoods and in the schools and in the churches, the hospital is"(40). Big Nurse places the blame on the inmates themselves: "You men are in the hospital," she says, "because of your proven inability to adjust to society"(145). Shuffling through the ward in a mental or drug-induced haze, staring vacant-eyed from wheelchair or Gurney bed, or cowering in rooms or hallways "like rabbits," these husks of men become fixtures in the surreal setting. In the communal bathroom, Bromden sees "faces all round . . . trapped screaming behind the mirrors"(12). Despite the obvious fact that little "fixing" of mistakes actually is accomplished, the ward continues to operate under Big Nurse as a "a smooth, accurate, precision-made machine" in accordance with the theory of the Therapeutic Community. "Our intention," Dr. Spivey explains, ". . . is to make this as much like our own democratic, free neighborhoods as possible—a little world Inside that is a made-to-scale prototype of the big world Outside that you will one day be taking your place in again"(48–49). The microcosmic-macrocosmic parallel that Dr. Spivey draws here is deeply ironic, of course, for in a series of glimpses into settings beyond the hospital walls, it becomes clear that mental health and genuine happiness are as rare outside as inside the cuckoo's nest.

The Outside

Like the inside, the outside is primarily a place of ridicule, intimidation, conformity, routine, and dehumanization. Enroute to the ocean, the members of the fishing expedition find themselves the objects of rude curiosity on the freeway when "the townspeople who were driving past on their way to work slow down to gawk at all the loonies in green uniforms"(199). At the service station, the attendants laugh at them and try to exploit them until McMurphy intervenes. Along the way, Bromden records the appearance of life on the outside:

> All up the coast I could see the signs of what the Combine had accomplished since I was last through this country, things like, for example—a *train* stopping at a station and laying a string of full-grown men in mirrored suits and machined hats, laying them like a hatch of identical insects, half-life things coming pht-pht-pht out of the last car, then hooting its electric whistle and moving on down the spoiled land to deposit another hatch.
>
> Or things like five thousand houses punched out identical by a machine and strung across the hills outside of town, so fresh from the factory they're still linked together like sausages. . . .
>
> . . . The houses looked so much alike that, time and time again, the kids went home by mistake to different houses and different families. Nobody ever noticed. (203–4)

Bromden's mixture of mechanical with natural imagery here suggests the encroachment of technology on nature, and his description documents the extent of conformity and dehumanization that has taken place outside. For Bromden, this is evidence of the influence of Big Nurse and her kind: "She's got to spend some time Outside. So she works with an eye to adjusting the Outside world too. Working alongside others like her who I call the 'Combine,' which is a huge organization that aims to adjust the Outside as well as she has the Inside . . ."(30). At the coast in Florence, the inmates are ridiculed by loafers on the dock and made to feel insignificant and helpless. From his high school days, Bromden recalls a field trip to a cotton mill with "all the humming and clicking and rattling of people and machinery, jerking around in a pattern" and "faces hypnotized by routine"(39). The point in every instance is made graphically clear: the Inside and the Outside are mirror images of painfully diminished lives.

The one exception in the outside setting is the natural environment. Bromden fondly remembers hunting birds and deer with his father in the Dalles and watching as a boy from the banks of the Columbia River as the men of his tribe speared salmon from the scaffolding at the falls. These are the memories that lure him back to nature when he escapes the ward imaginatively through a pastoral picture on the wall:

> There's a path running down through the aspen, and I push my broom down the path a ways and sit down on a rock and look back out through the frame at that visiting doctor talking with the residents. I can see him stabbing some point in the palm of his hand with his finger, but I can't hear what he says because of the crash of the cold, frothy stream coming down out of the rocks. I can smell the snow in the wind where it blows down off the peaks, I can see mole burrows humping along under the grass and buffalo weed. It's a real nice place to stretch your legs and take it easy. (112)

This scene anticipates the later scene when Bromden's senses come alive as he looks from inside to outside through a real window in the ward at the young dog sniffing digger squirrel holes and frolicking in the grass and moonlight before following the wild geese out of sight and thus prefiguring the ultimate direction of Bromden's escape from the hospital. Despite the unpleasantness of the fishing crew's trip to the coast, the natural scene was a pleasure to Bromden: "It was a fine woodsmoked autumn day, full of the sound of kids punting footballs and the putter of small airplanes, and everybody should've been happy just being outside in it"(199). And finally, the sea provides beauty, space, and peace: "When we passed the last point of the jetty and the last black rock, I could feel a great calmness creep over me, and calmness that increased the farther we left land behind us"(208). Although Bromden has come to fear the swimming-pool water on the Inside—

"The pool always scared me; I was always afraid I'd step in over my head and drown"(147)—he feels, like Huck Finn on the river, free and safe on the water on the Outside. It is in this setting that McMurphy, with nature's help, will work his restorative magic on Bromden and the others.

5

PLOT

Cuckoo's Nest is formally divided into four sections, but the overall structure of the novel answers neatly to the exposition-complication-climax-falling action-resolution pattern of traditional fiction. Discovery and reversal are central devices in the development of the plot, and within each of the four sections there are structural dynamics that at once mark the boundaries of the individual dramatic units, reflect the overall narrative strategy, and advance the movement of the main plot. Each part begins with a conflict between McMurphy and Big Nurse over some specific issue and ends with McMurphy triumphant, though in part 4 his triumph is spiritual only. The conflict between McMurphy and Big Nurse embodies the freedom-versus-repression theme while McMurphy's struggle to restore the inmates to manhood embodies the failure-of-self-reliance theme. McMurphy's growth from con man to hero to messiah is paralleled by Bromden's growth from coward to hero. In the falling action of part 4, this parallel pattern becomes chiasmic, however, for as McMurphy grows weaker, Bromden grows stronger. The full restoration of Bromden's humanity at the end serves as the redemption for McMurphy's sacrifice of his life for others and underscores the major theme that people can cope with the absurdities of life if they will cultivate the will and the courage to do so.

Part 1 of the novel provides the exposition, the initial complications, and what functions as a preliminary climax. The expository action includes the abrupt self-introduction of Bromden as narrator, his reflections on some war history as antecedent action, his observations on personalities and procedures, and his account of a new, atypical admission—McMurphy. McMurphy is initiated into the war experience primarily by his attendance at a Group Meeting of the Therapeutic Community, where he discovers in amazement the extent of Big Nurse's power and the degree to which the men submit to it. In instinctual responses to what he perceives as an unnatural balance of power, he wagers the men that he can shake Nurse Ratched's control within a week. The bet pits McMurphy formally against Big Nurse over the central issue of control and thus ends the expository section. In the complications that follow, McMurphy makes points as he shocks Big Nurse with his singing and whale shorts but suffers a setback when he fails to rally the men against her in the first TV vote. He seems to lose again when he fails to lift the symbolic "control" panel in the tub room, but his strategically designed "failure" bears fruit when the men, inspired by his superhuman effort at "uplifting" with the control panel, support him in the second TV vote and join him in defiance of Big Nurse in front of the blanked-out TV, winning his bet for him because Big Nurse, out of control, is "hollering and squealing at the back of their heads about discipline and order and recriminations . . . "(128). For their good and his gain, McMurphy defeats Big Nurse in a scene that concludes part 1 and functions in the overall plot as the first victory in McMurphy's evolving mission to assist the inmates and resist the Combine.

In part 2 the conflict between McMurphy and Nurse Ratched is intensified, and he has to make the difficult choice between self-interest and brotherhood, between safety and danger. The meeting of the medical staff that opens the section parallels the meeting of the inmates over the bet that opened part 1, so that at the beginning of part 2 the position of McMurphy's antagonist is presented, and she is confident that his self-interest will bring him into line: "As a psychopath," she says, "he's much too fond of a Mr. Randle Patrick McMurphy to subject him to any needless danger"(136). Her confidence is bolstered by knowledge that McMurphy does not share: "Keep in mind," she reminds the staff in a statement that is expository for this section, "that Mr. McMurphy is committed. The length of time he spends in this hospital is entirely up to us"(137). In the ensuing complication, McMurphy learns—significantly from the "lifeguard"—the consequences of being committed. This discovery leads McMurphy to a temporary reversal in his war with Nurse Ratched. In demonstration that he certainly is human and that his survival is important to him, he begins to look out for himself and ignore the men. He will not help a hydrocephalous patient who has fallen in a footbath. He does his work without badgering Big Nurse. He refuses to support Cheswick on the cigarette issue. He submits to Big Nurse and the imperatives of self-interest. However, Cheswick's suicide in the swimming pool, Sefelt's epileptic seizure in the cafeteria from nonmedication, and, most important, the confession from Harding and others that they are voluntary patients and not committed lead McMurphy, despite his self-interest, to the discovery of the need for him to share strength with the weak men around him. This discovery awakens his compassion and stirs the champion in him, and in a reversal that is a delayed tribute to Cheswick and a renewal of the struggle for the men and against the Combine, he shatters the glass in the Nurses' Station, retrieves his cigarettes, and re-establishes his status as a contender for control. This intense scene concludes part 2 in another preliminary climax and advances McMurphy's rise to heroism and Bromden's move toward clarity. "The ringing that was in my head had stopped"(173), Bromden declares after McMurphy's return to the fray.

In part 3 the pace of the rising action accelerates toward the fishing scene, which serves dually as the climax of this section and the major dramatic climax of the novel. The struggle between McMurphy and Nurse Ratched here goes mainly his way, for he and the inmates are energized by his apparent growing dominance over her. She can offer only token resistance to his extensions of power. Over her objections, he organizes a basketball team with Dr. Spivey's approval because it has "therapeutic value." The team practices in the hallways, disrupting the routines of the ward. Big Nurse in response denies two of McMurphy's requests for leave time, the first an Unaccompanied Leave, the second an Accompanied Leave with a "twitch" from Portland. In response to her denials, McMurphy "accidentally" breaks the glass in the Nurses' Station again: "When did they sneak that danged glass in there? Why that thing is a *menace!*"(176). McMurphy's team loses the basketball game against the aides, but McMurphy insouciantly bloodies Washington's nose with his elbow during official play and gets away with it. McMurphy resumes his badgering of Big Nurse with obscene notes in the latrine and deflects her reprimands with sexual innuendoes. Following McMurphy's lead, the inmates extend the rebellion. Harding flirts with the student nurses, Billy Bibbit stops writing in the log book, and Scanlon breaks the glass in the Nurses' Station with the basketball, shattering Nurse Ratched's insularity for a third time. McMurphy's third request for Accompanied Leave with "two sweet old aunts" is approved in staff meeting, then, because the chaperones seem respectable and other patients will be involved in the therapeutic expedition.

The fishing trip is therapeutic, of course, but not in terms that Nurse Ratched could approve, for it frees the men physically and symbolically from the clutches of the Combine. With its subplots and conflicts, this episode is a little plot within a larger plot but sharing a common climax. Nurse Ratched opposes the trip, naturally, and tries to scuttle it by posting newspaper clippings on the bulletin board about rough seas and shipwrecks on the coast. McMurphy has to counter her appeals to fear with his own appeals to courage in order to fill out his crew. In the important subplot, he discovers that Bromden can speak, and he learns of the external conditions that caused this huge Indian to feel small and to feign deafness and dumbness as a psychological defense against the Combine that he watched destroy his father, Chief Tee Ah Millatoona, The-Pine-That-Stands-Tallest-on-the-Mountain. McMurphy's response to this new discovery is to promise to effect a reversal in Bromden by making him "big" again, a process McMurphy begins by giving Bromden an erection through the spinning of erotic fantasies starring the Chief as a new superstud.

Plot

The complications in part 3 intensify from the trivial matters of arranging a second car and signing on Dr. Spivey as the final crew member to the more troublesome matters of exposing the inmates to stultifying external forces and keeping their spirits high. The first conflict on the outside occurs in the service station, where the attendants mock Dr. Spivey and the patients from the hospital until McMurphy intimidates them in turn and goes to an adjoining store to buy beer. The discovery of the effectiveness of McMurphy's courage on the outside as well as on the inside inspires the crew to an immediate reversal of attitude and behavior:

> By the time he got back everybody was feeling cocky as fighting roosters and calling orders to the service-station guys to check the air in the spare and wipe the windows and scratch that bird dropping off the hood if you please, just like we owned the show.(202)

The next conflict occurs on the docks, where the loafers make insulting remarks about Candy's sexual appeal, the appearance of the inmates, and their apparent impotence and helplessness. Without McMurphy, the men suffer another reversal and return to their fearful, diminished selves. They simply endure the humiliation in silence until McMurphy emerges from the Captain's office and rushes them all out to sea. At this point, McMurphy's people are so shrunken by intimidation and shame as to be barely recognizable as human, but once at sea McMurphy succeeds in restoring them to normal size and natural form.

The fishing scene is both the climax of part 3 and the major climax of the novel. Away from the embarrassing public scrutiny and under the influence of McMurphy, the men relax, drink beer, and enjoy Candy's feminine presence, the sunshine, the open sea, the fellowship, and the freedom. They catch fish, and finally they can open up and laugh:

> It started slow and pumped itself full, swelling the men bigger and bigger. I watched, part of them, laughing with them—and

somehow not with them. I was off the boat, blown up off the water and skating the wind with those black birds, high above myself, and I could look down and see myself and the rest of the guys, see the boat rocking there in the middle of those diving birds, see McMurphy surrounded by his dozen people, and watch them, us, swinging a laughter that rang out on the water in ever-widening circles, farther and farther, until it crashed up on beaches all over the coast, on beaches all over all coasts, in wave after wave after wave. (212)

During the scene, McMurphy denies his help to the men to force them to discover that they can help themselves. The discovery makes them bigger. McMurphy allows Billy, Harding, and George the choice of making the trip to shore heroically unprotected by life preservers when the crew discover that they are three life jackets short. That small degree of heroism makes them bigger. The laughter inflates them all, but biggest of all is Bromden, who soars above the scene as the most dramatic evidence of McMurphy's restorative powers. Although during the trip back to the hospital McMurphy reveals the strain he is under as a builder of confidence and uplifter of spirits, he has demonstrated in this powerful scene that he qualifies as the messianic figure that Ellis had called for earlier, a "fisher of men"(198).

Part 4 of the novel contains the falling action and the resolution, and in this part of the narrative Bromden and McMurphy gradually exchange positions. The designation "falling action" here means not a loss of narrative interest but only a movement away from climax toward denouement, for this section maintains all the way to the end a dramatic intensity equal in the key scenes to the new line of action marked by the climactic fishing scene. The exposition in part 4 consists of Big Nurse's attempts to discredit McMurphy in the eyes of the men by posting the financial accounts of the Acutes and posing pointed questions to them about the motives behind McMurphy's obviously profitable altruism: "he seems to do things," she says, "without thinking of himself at all, as if he were a martyr or a saint. Would anyone venture that Mr. McMurphy was a saint? . . . No, not a saint *or* a martyr. Here. Shall we examine a cross section of this man's philanthropy?"(222). In questioning McMurphy's integrity, Big Nurse intensifies her personal contest with him yet again, but in introducing, even ironically, the terms *saint* and *martyr,* she provides the standards by which McMurphy will in the end be rightly judged and thus undercuts her own position. In the scenes of complication that follow this exposition, the issue of McMurphy's integrity is shown to be intimately joined to the continued growth of the inmates, again especially to Bromden, who must rise to the challenge when McMurphy's self-chosen martyrdom leaves space for a new hero.

Nurse Ratched succeeds for a while in arousing the suspicions of the men against McMurphy, even with Billy and Bromden, his staunchest allies. Billy is dismayed to discover that McMurphy intends to make money off of the "date" he has arranged for Billy with Candy, and Bromden is shocked to be used by McMurphy to fleece the men in the tub room with the wager over Bromden's ability to lift the control panel. Although McMurphy's aim in the episode is mainly to demonstrate to the Chief his renewed strength, he also wishes to show the inmates solid evidence of one of their own whose "bigness" has been restored. To assure their attention, McMurphy again uses the gambit of a wager. Bromden is the primary beneficiary here, but all he can see, along with the others, is a successful gambler. "You're always . . . *winning* things"(226), Bromden says, fighting tears. With the weariness of one who is deeply drained and misunderstood, McMurphy can only reply, "'Winning, for Christsakes,' he said with his eyes closed 'Hoo boy, winning'"(227). Big Nurse appears clearly in the ascendancy here, with even Billy and Bromden doubting McMurphy's motives.

To restore his credibility and character in the eyes of the men and thus to continue to minister to their need for strength, McMurphy must rise to ever greater exertions in his increasingly dangerous struggle against Big Nurse and the Combine. And Bromden, to validate his resurgent manhood, must shoulder an increasing share of McMurphy's burden. The transfer of power between these two occurs over a series of scenes in part 4 from the fight in the shower to McMurphy's attack on Big Nurse, a series that constitutes a kind of extended climax for part 4 and an intense falling action for the overall plot.

Big Nurse sets up the incident in the shower by devising a "cautionary cleansing" for the fishermen that is clearly punitive in nature, but Washington, the black aid whose nose McMurphy smashed in the basketball game, provokes the fight by taunting George, the Swedish clean-freak, with the foul-smelling tube of disinfectant. Ostensibly taunting the Swede, Washington is really taunting McMurphy. To defend George, McMurphy must put himself at risk, not only in the fight, but in its consequences, win or lose. He chooses to do so anyway to continue his commitment to the men. His defeat of Washington leads the men to a discovery: "we'd all been wrong about McMurphy"(228), and that discovery leads to a reversal. In support of McMurphy, the inmates break ranks; "that neat, silent line of nude men changed into a yelling circle, limbs and bodies knitting in a ring of flesh"(230), and when Warren leaps on McMurphy's back, the Chief uses his new strength and "picked him off and threw him in the shower. He was full of tubes; he didn't weight more 'n ten or fifteen pounds"(231). From this point on, the men entertain no doubts about the character of McMurphy or his motives, and Bromden naturally functions as his faithful thane and disciple. Together they survive the EST treatment that Big Nurse prescribes as punishment for their misbehavior. McMurphy receives more treatments than Bromden, however, in proportion to his more vocal defiance and thus, as Bromden reports, pays a higher price than he wishes to acknowledge: "But every time that loudspeaker called for him to forgo breakfast and prepare to walk to Building One, the muscles in his jaw went taut and his whole face drained of color, looking thin and scared—the face I had seen reflected in the windshield on the trip back from the coast"(243). The strength that McMurphy is losing devolves on Bromden, along with leadership, as he becomes the spokesman in the ward for the resistance:

> I told them all I could, and nobody seemed to think a thing about
> me all of a sudden talking with people—a guy who'd been consid-

ered deaf and dumb as far back as they'd known him, talking, listening, just like anybody. I told them everything that they'd heard was true, and tossed in a few stories of my own. (243)

Bromden shows himself in this scene to be fully emergent, from the fog, from feigned deafness and dumbness, from fear—a living testament to McMurphy's "bigness" therapy.

The party on the ward, then, celebrates Bromden's rebirth and prefigures McMurphy's demise. The night is filled with celebration, revelry, laughter, and lovemaking. The morning brings discovery: McMurphy and Sandy in bed "like two tired little kids," Billy and Candy in flagrante delicto, and the ward in a shambles of debauchery and broken rules. Nurse Ratched's retaliation is to shame Billy to suicide. In the obligatory scene that ends the falling action and represents the culmination of McMurphy's conflict with Big Nurse, McMurphy retaliates for Billy's death by attacking Big Nurse in righteous anger, revealing the breasts she has tried to hide, and genuinely trying to kill her. McMurphy pulls out all the stops in this scene, for he knows his act can lead to his own death; the sound he makes as he is subdued "is like the last sound the treed and shot and falling animal makes as the dogs get him, when he doesn't care any more about anything but himself and his dying"(267).

The resolution of the plot in part 4 and the whole novel is dominated by Bromden, who must decide what to do on his own when McMurphy's lobotomized body is wheeled back into the ward on a Gurney bed. McMurphy's vacuous face and the shell that was once a vibrant man lead Bromden quickly to a decision on grounds respectful to McMurphy and to other men who might be assigned later to the ward: "I was only sure of one thing," Bromden reasons: "he wouldn't have left something like that sit there in the day room with his name tacked on it for twenty or thirty years so the Big Nurse could use it as an example of what can happen if you buck the system. I was sure of that"(270). In a gesture of love, Bromden smothers McMurphy and then with a strength born of grief, anger, resolve, and a renewed sense of possibility, he lifts the symbolic control panel and smashes his way out of the cuckoo's nest. It is an act set up by McMurphy in the tub-room wager, and it is the final evidence of Bromden's full growth to heroism under McMurphy's tutelage. Following the direction taken by the wild geese and the young dog he had seen earlier on the moonlit night, Bromden heads for freedom and its attendant dangers to try to do for others what McMurphy has done for him. He moves from the microcosm of the ward toward the macrocosm of the tribal falls on the government's new hydroelectric dam "to see if there's any of the guys I used to know back in the village who haven't drunk themselves goofy"(272); he seeks in the spirit of McMurphy to share his strength as an aid to the weak, to employ his courage in the cause of sanity and justice, and to reduce the level of absurdity in the world. That is the new basis of stability concluding the plot of the novel.

6

CHARACTERIZATION

Principal Characters

The carefully constructed plot of *Cuckoo's Nest* demonstrates that Kesey assigns a high priority to the structural design of his story, although he is not Aristotelian enough to consider plot more important than other major literary devices. Kesey seems closer to the position that Henry James described in "The Art of Fiction" in the form of two central questions: "What is character but the determination of incident? What is incident but the illustration of character?" James argues here, interrogatively, for the organic unity of plot and character, but he sees character as the key element. Kesey's fiction, too, is character based. When an interviewer asked Kesey once how he felt about the intricacy of Robbe-Grillet's plotting and point of view in the film *Last Year at Marienbad,* he revealed in his reply a resistance to the subjugation in art of people to technique: "That excited me as a *device* but bored me very much as a *movie.* He's lost the sense of people in his work, that's the trouble. I don't think you can veer very far from human problems and emotions and still suck the reader into turning the page."[20] The "sense of people" is therefore central to *Cuckoo's Nest* as it is to the rest of Kesey's fiction, and the spectrum of characterization in the novel runs from flat, stereotypical figures like Big Nurse, who is presented mainly through action and dialogue, to round, complex figures like Bromden, who is presented mainly through an interior monologue. But flat or round, static or dynamic, exterior or interior in presentation, all of the characters come alive and, in Faulkner's terminology for his own best creations, "stand up and cast a shadow."

As McMurphy's antagonist and the agent of the Combine, Big Nurse casts a very big shadow indeed. She is the villain of the piece, and Kesey makes no attempt to complicate her character or mitigate her villainy in her interactions with the men on the ward. In his address in 1981 to the Associated Writing Programs Conference in Seattle, Kesey said, "A good story needs a good villain—one that is evil, not just bad"—and the writer must find a way to "draw a bead" on that character or quality.[21] Kesey uses simple caricature to draw a bead on Big Nurse as the embodiment of oppression. In the eyes of Bromden, McMurphy, and the others who are aware enough to form judgments, she is simply the Enemy, the focal point of their fears, frustrations, and angers. In the larger rhetoric of the novel as a whole, however—that is, beyond the purview of the inmates—Nurse Ratched appears as another product shaped by the Combine. Her compulsiveness for order, control, power, and punishment has been conditioned in her as the guardian of the ward by the same forces that have misshapen the inmates and placed them under her care. She is in this light as much a victim as a victimizer, but she does not see herself as a victim, and she generates no sympathy because Kesey does not allow her to grow beyond caricature. Her rigid inhumanity provides a useful contrast by which to witness the painful groping toward humanity— and beyond caricature—of the other principal characters.

As an ex-army nurse accustomed to regimentation and inflexible routine, Big Nurse has come to value order for its own sake, and her rage for order has been enacted at the expense of her womanhood and her natural relationship to the world. Although she functions as an Orwellian Big Brother for the Combine, nature has endowed her with an ample bosom designed for nurturing and comforting. Her nickname and her physique suggest an extraordinary capacity for suckling children and sustaining life, but she has resisted that function and tries to hide her breasts behind tight, stiffly starched uniforms. The men comment on the trait often. "A mistake was made somehow in manufacturing," says Bromden, "putting those big, womanly breasts on what would of otherwise been a perfect work, and you can see how bitter she is about it"(11). Harding comments similarly to McMurphy: "And in spite of all her attempts to *conceal* them, in that sexless get-up, you can still make out the evidence of some rather extraordinary breasts"(66). McMurphy even has the audacity to ask her "just what was the actual inch-by-inch measurement on them great big ol' breasts that she did her best to conceal but never could," but as Bromden reports, "she walked right on past, ignoring him just like she chose to ignore the way nature had tagged her with those outsized badges of femininity, just like she was above him, and sex, and everything else that's weak and of the flesh"(138). To deny her sexuality is to deny her humanity. In the terms of Bromden's analysis here, she is guilty of a form of hubris, trying to rise above the weakness of the merely mortal. To McMurphy, such a denial is a form of insult, for in refusing to be a natural woman, Nurse Ratched obviates McMurphy's role as a natural man, a practice that helps to account in part for the nature of his final attack on her.

The extent to which Big Nurse has succeeded in dehumanizing herself is clear from the mechanical and animalistic forms she assumes in the eyes of others. To Bromden, the tips of her fingers are a "Funny orange. Like the tip of a soldering iron"(10). In her purse "there's no compact or lipstick or woman stuff, she's got that bag full of a thousand parts she aims to use in her duties today—wheels and gears, cogs polished to a hard glitter"(10). In anger at the aides, she becomes a thundering eighteen-wheeler:

> She works the hinges in her elbows and fingers, I hear a small squeak. She starts moving, and I get back against the wall, and when she rumbles past she's already big as a truck, trailing that wicker bag behind in her exhaust like a semi behind a Jimmy Diesel. Her lips are parted, and her smile's going out before her like a radiator grill. I can smell the hot oil and magneto spark when she

goes past, and every step hits the floor she blows up a size bigger, blowing and puffing, roll down anything in her path! (87)

Bromden's hyperbolic magnification of Nurse Ratched here reveals his distorted sense of her power and his own insignificance, but his impressionistic descriptions of her dehumanized nature are supported by the assessments Bromden reports from others. To McMurphy, Big Nurse is a "ball cutter" who is "big as a damn barn and tough as knife metal"(57). Cheswick says that Big Nurse "grinds our noses in our mistakes"(59) during Group Meetings. For Harding, Nurse Ratched is a predator among prey: ". . . we're not in here *because* we are rabbits—we'd be rabbits wherever we were—we're all in here because we can't *adjust* to our rabbithood. We *need* a good strong wolf like the nurse to teach us our place"(61). Every instance, and there are many others, gives evidence of the distance from human form and impulse Big Nurse has traveled in the interest of what she has been led to believe is orderly and right.

The order by which she defines herself is the same order she seeks to achieve in the ward:

> The Big Nurse tends to get real put out if something keeps her outfit from running like a smooth, accurate, precision-made machine. The slightest thing messy or out of kilter or in the way ties her into a little white knot of tight-smiled fury. She walks around with that same doll smile crimped between her chin and her nose and that same calm whir coming from her eyes, but down inside of her she's tense as steel. I know, I can feel it. And she don't relax a hair till she gets the nuisance attended to—what she calls "adjusted to surroundings." (30)

Bromden's exterior view poses as an interior one in this analysis in what may appear to be a straining of narrative perspective, but since only his voice tells the tale, his speculations provide the only access to Big Nurse's motives. Reliable or not—and that issue will be explored in Chapter 8, Point of View—Bromden describes Big Nurse's actions and interprets her intentions, values, and aspirations: "What she dreams of there in the center of those wires," Bromden imagines, "is a world of precision, efficiency, and tidiness like a pocket watch with a glass back, where the schedule is unbreakable and all the patients who aren't Outside, obedient under her beam, are wheelchair Chronics with catheter tubes run direct from every pantleg to the sewer under the floor"(30). What Bromden perceives in Nurse Ratched is a slave to order, one who is willing to sacrifice all vestiges of femininity, compassion, and tolerance in order to impose her narrow conception on the little world she oversees.

To that end, the acquisition and maintenance of control and the exercise of power are of central importance to Nurse Ratched. She chooses nurses for her staff on the basis of their malleability. With the help of her friend the supervisor of the hospital, she arranges for a physician on the ward who is impractical and susceptible to intimidation; Dr. Spivey is her puppet. She selects aides whose exposure to social injustice and racism on the Outside has created in them an unfocused hate that is a constant source of energy. She channels that hate and that energy into a monitoring system of retaliatory discipline on the Inside. The aides become an extension of her compulsion for order and the physical manifestations of her power: "They are in contact on a high-voltage wave length of hate, and the black boys are out there performing her bidding before she even thinks it"(32). She controls the inmates with rigid routines, pills, the log book, Group Therapy, Electro-Shock Therapy, and issue-specific punishments that are really muscle-flexing masquerading as socially instructive correction: "At some time—perhaps in your childhood—you may have been allowed to get away with flouting the rules of society. When you broke a rule you knew it. You wanted to be dealt with, *needed* it, but the punishment did not come. That foolish lenience on the part of your parents may have been the germ that grew into your present illness. I tell you this hoping you will understand that it is *entirely for your own good* that we enforce discipline and order"(171).

McMurphy, of course, is the greatest threat to discipline and order that Big Nurse has to confront on the ward, and she sees him, with his free-spirited indifference to her methodology and to her dreams of order, as her natural antagonist and a serious danger to the Combine she serves. She spells out the danger to Nurse Flinn: "Sometimes a manipulator's own ends are simply the actual *disruption* of the ward for the sake of disruption. There are such people in our society. A manipulator can influence the other patients and disrupt them to such an extent that it may take months to get everything running smooth once more"(29). Driven by this misperception of McMurphy's motives and her own opposite compulsion to avoid disruption at all costs, she escalates her punishments for his various misdemeanors, from rest-room-cleaning detail to Electro-Shock Therapy to lobotomy, but it is clear that the punishment in every case is designed to protect her power, not to improve McMurphy's character, though that is the jus-tification she offers for it. "Randle," she coos as she assigns him to EST, "we are trying to help you"(236). When she shames Billy Bibbit into committing suicide and then tries to shift the blame to Mc-Murphy, her language reveals the magnitude of the threat she perceives him to be: "I hope you're finally satisfied. Playing with human lives— gambling with human lives—as if you thought yourself to be a *God!*"(266). The activities and the deific power she ascribes to McMurphy are actually her own in practice, and the hysteria in her voice reveals the extent to which McMurphy threatens both and thus in her eyes justifies the lobotomy that cancels McMurphy's threat. When she returns to the ward after McMurphy's assault, she is wounded but unchanged. She may have lost a battle, but the war and the ward go on, and she sees herself, despite residual flare-ups from the few remaining members of McMurphy's crew, as the continuing crusader for order. As such, she remains a flat character who is as close to an Elizabethan humours figure* as one can find in contemporary fiction.

*Drawing on medieval theories about the four basic liquids of the human body (blood, phlegm, yellow bile, and black bile), the Elizabethans believed that mental and physical health depended on a balance of the "humours," these fundamental fluids, as they coursed through the human anatomy. An imbalance created a recog-nizable type of behavior. Because she is irascible, impatient, stubbornly single-minded, and vindictive, Big Nurse is a choleric figure whose personality is determined by a dominance of yellow bile in her system, and the Combine reinforces her militant predisposition.

By contrast with Big Nurse as antagonist, McMurphy as protagonist is fully developed, and the power in his characterization inheres in his dramatic evolution from con man to messianic martyr. According to the official record, which Big Nurse hands to Dr. Spivey "like she's got a man folded up inside that yellow paper and can pass him on to be looked over"(45), McMurphy is, in the main, a disorderly type:

> McMurry, Randle Patrick. Committed by the state from the Pendleton Farm for Correction. For diagnosis and possible treatment. Thirty-five years old. Never married. Distinguished Service Cross in Korea, for leading an escape from a Communist prison camp. A dishonorable discharge, afterward, for insubordination. Followed by a history of street brawls and barroom fights and a series of arrests for Drunkenness, Assault and Battery, Disturbing the Peace, re*peated* gambling, and one arrest—for Rape. (44)

With its evidence of prideful individualism and disrespect for order and authority, this record sets off the complete alarm system in the psyche of Big Nurse, the Combine's regional guardian of order. She simply ignores his war heroism as a part that does not fit the larger pattern, but she ignores it at her peril, for this early evidence of McMurphy's commitment to human freedom is a seed that will be nurtured into a tree in his relations with the men in the cuckoo's nest and will eventually bear the fruit of their freedom before it expires from the effort.

McMurphy enters the ward, however, on a lark and confesses candidly that he is seeking a form of incarceration less demanding than the Pendleton Work Farm:

> What happened, you see, was I got in a couple of hassles at the work farm, to tell the pure truth, and the court ruled that I'm a psychopath. And do you think I'm gonna argue with the court? Shoo, you can bet your bottom dollar I don't. If it gets me outta those damn pea fields I'll be whatever their little heart desires, be it

psychopath or mad dog or werewolf, because I don't care if I never see another weedin' hoe to my dying day. (17–18)

At this point, McMurphy's motives indicate pure self-interest, and he revels in the soft life he has arranged for himself. "Look at me now," he exults, "bacon, toast, butter, eggs—coffee the little honey in the kitchen even asks me if I like it black or white thank you—and a great! big! cold glass of orange juice. Why you couldn't *pay* me to leave this place!"(93). Part of this stagy speech is tongue-in-cheek, but it is also a genuine admission of the comparative ease he is enjoying in new surroundings. As a contrast, he is also enjoying the company of mental patients over criminals, and his kidding of the men—with Harding as "Bull Goose Loony" or Billy as "Billy 'Club' Bibbit"—is as much for his own entertainment as for their edification.

McMurphy is also candid with the men about his activities as a hustler and a gambler. He even explains to them the psychology of being a successful con man: "The secret of being a top-notch con man is being able to know what the mark *wants* and how to make him think he's getting it"(74). He employs his psychology on the ward, for his con man's eye picks out many "marks" whose wants are painfully self-evident. Billy wants self-confidence, Harding wants manhood. Sefelt wants health, Cheswick wants toughness, Bromden wants clarity and growth, and so on through an inventory as numerous as the men in the hospital. They all want freedom and respect. They are losers who want to be winners. While filling his own pockets, McMurphy caters to these desires in small ways—backing up Cheswick in his machismo posturing, for example, or casting Harding in the role of a leader, or spinning fantasy tales of sexual adventures starring Billy or Bromden, or making them all winners in set-up card games: "He let them win, and every one of us watching the game knows it. So do the players. But there still isn't a man raking his pile of cigarettes . . . that doesn't have a smirk on his face like he's the toughest gambler on the whole Mississippi" (75). Letting them win is McMurphy's strategy for eventually winning himself, but he is also candid about that: "I'm starting level with you. I'm a gambler, and I'm not in the habit of losing"(68). But neither his candor nor his self-interest can save him from progressive involvement with these men, for given his strength and essential compassion, their weakness and need ensnare him in a voluntary but ineluctable moral growth. In a variation on the Heraclitean formula, their characters become his fate. When the needs of the "mark" take precedence over the importance of his own gain in the eyes of the con man himself, then the hustler himself has been hustled in a sense, for he has become something else, a good man.

McMurphy briefly resists this transformation in the name of his freedom and survival, but his basic good nature, his fierce opposition to tyranny, and his growing affection for the inmates compel him to support or defend them again and again.

The first time that he actually places himself at risk with the Big Nurse is in the wager with the men over the issue of control. McMurphy bets that he can "Bug her till she comes apart at those neat little seams, and shows, just one time, she isn't so unbeatable as you think"(69). He embarks on this venture in part to respond to the men's need for a challenger to Big Nurse, but mainly to exercise his own personal power to feather his own nest, yet he is careful to learn the boundaries of permissible effrontery: "What I want to know," he asks Harding before advancing the wager, "is am I safe to try to beat her at her own game? If I come on nice as pie to her, whatever else I in-sinuate, she ain't gonna get in a tizzy and have me electrocuted?"(68). McMurphy's spectacular success in winning this bet in the second TV vote, and in the defiant scene in front of the television set, allows him to make his money and protect his flanks, but it also draws him deeper into his engagement with the inmates and their various weaknesses. Without any possibility of financial gain for himself, he exerts greater efforts to draw the men out: "Whack his leg and throw back his head and laugh and laugh, digging his thumb into the ribs of whoever was sitting next to him, trying to get him to laugh too"(139). The campaign *against* Big Nurse, then, becomes more and more a campaign *for* the inmates. Feeding off of their approbation, McMurphy seems increasingly less concerned about his own safety.

However, when McMurphy learns from the lifeguard that Big

Nurse can extend his sentence indefinitely because he is one of the "committed" inmates, he reverts to self-interested behavior and withdraws from the struggle against Big Nurse and for the men. This withdrawal is important in the characterization of McMurphy because it shows that he values his own life, that he is human and not a superman. The explanation for his change of heart that he offers to Harding bears no traces of heroism—"Just because I don't like her ain't a sign I'm gonna bug her into adding another year or so to my sentence. You got to swallow your pride sometimes and keep an eye out for old Number One"(166)—and he chides the men for taking advantage of him:

> Why should it be me goes to bat at these meetings over these piddling little gripes about keeping the dorm door open and about cigarettes in the Nurses' Station? I couldn't figure it at first, why you guys were coming to me like I was some kind of savior. Then I just happened to find out about the way nurses have the big say as to who gets discharged and who doesn't. And I got wise awful damned fast, I said, "Why, those slippery bastards have *conned* me, snowed me into holding their bag. If that don't beat all, conned ol' R. P. McMurphy." He tips his head back and grins at the line of us on the bench. "Well, I don't mean nothing personal, you understand, buddies, but screw that noise. I want out of here just as much as the rest of you. I got just as much to lose hassling that old buzzard as *you* do." (166–67)

This self-justifying speech accounts for McMurphy's good behavior on the ward, his new show of respect for Nurse Ratched, and his decision to look out for "old Number One," but it is not a posture he can maintain for long.

Discoveries that McMurphy makes in several key scenes lead him to the gradual abandonment of his self-interested withdrawal from the inmates and the war with Nurse Ratched. Cheswick's suicide and Bromden's descent into his protective fog teach McMurphy the depths of desperation in the ward. Sefelt's epileptic seizure from nonmedication and Harding's destructive visit from his wife show McMurphy the extent of confusion in the ward. Big Nurse's unrelenting pressures demonstrate the ubiquitous danger in the ward. Martini's claim for the faces all around—"Hold it a minute. They need you to see thum"(161)—reveals the magnitude of their need. And, most compelling of all, Harding's startling revelation that most of the men are there voluntarily—"Not many commitments in the whole hospital. No, not many at all"(167)—indicates both the urgency for action and the absence of anyone to act, except McMurphy himself. "Are you guys *bullshitting* me?"(167) he asks in baffled rage. Although he loves his life, McMurphy loves freedom and hates tyranny more, and thus is brought to a moment of awful decision. Bromden monitors his *agon* in the walk back from Building One after the emotional scene over commitment with Harding, Billy, and the others: ". . . I could see that there was some thought he was worrying over in his mind like a dog worries at a hole he don't know what's down, one voice saying, Dog, that hole is none of your affair—it's too big and too black and there's a spoor all over the place says bears or something just as bad. And some other voice coming like a sharp whisper out of way back in his breed, not a smart voice, nothing cagey about it, saying *Sic* 'im, dog, *sic* 'im!"(169). The prudent voice of self-interest contends here in McMurphy's mind with the heroic voice of risky adventure. The voice of the champion prevails, a "sharp whisper out of way back in his breed," and McMurphy indicates his intentions when he asks the aide to stop at the canteen for cigarettes because he plans "to do a lot of smokin' "(170). He realizes his intentions and resumes his role as defender of freedom when he breaks the glass in the Nurses' Station in defiance of the cigarette rationing and the newly instituted tub-room deprivation. From this point on, McMurphy is truly "committed," but not to dependency on Big Nurse for his freedom. His commitment—and it deepens with every punitive move that Big Nurse makes—is to the salvation of the men, whatever the personal costs.

The preparation for this commitment is supplied in the earlier willingness of McMurphy to risk his life for the freedom of others, the act for which he won the Distinguished Service Cross in Korea. The execution of the commitment involves McMurphy in coaching a basketball team, becoming the confidant and mentor of Bromden, defending the inmates against insult and hostility at the service station and on the docks, leading his people to liberation and laughter on the fishing trip, after which he shows to Bromden a face "dreadfully tired and strained and *frantic,* like there wasn't enough time left for something he had to do"(218), protecting George and the cause of human dignity in the shower fight, leading Billy to the joys of sex, inspiring the beleaguered men on Disturbed with his continued defiance after each of his EST treatments, and, finally, attacking Big Nurse in a culmination of his mission to risk all for others. In her charge that McMurphy rather than she herself is responsible for Billy's death and in her suggestion that McMurphy has been playing "God" with the lives of others, Big Nurse brings down an Old Testament wrath on herself, for McMurphy in his angry attack seeks simply a life for a life in accordance with ancient justice. In stripping her to the waist, McMurphy does not intend a rape, as some readers suppose, but only to reveal the emblems of a nurturing female nature to which Nurse Ratched has been unfaithful. His act is that of "a sane, willful, dogged man performing a hard duty that finally just had to be done, like it or not"(267).

In thoughtful retrospect, Bromden offers an explanation for the scope of McMurphy's commitment:

> I've given what happened next a good lot of thought, and I've come around to thinking that it was bound to be and would have happened in one way or another, at this time or that, even if Mr. Turkle had got McMurphy and the two girls up and off the ward like was planned. The Big Nurse would have found out some way what had gone on, maybe just by the look on Billy's face, and she'd have done the same as she did whether McMurphy was still around or not. And Billy would have done what he did, and McMurphy would have heard about it and come back.
>
> Would have *had* to come back, because he could no more have sat around outside the hospital, playing poker in Carson City or Reno or someplace, let the Big Nurse have the last move and get the last play, than he could have let her get by with it right under

his nose. It was like he'd signed on for the whole game and there wasn't any way of him breaking his contract. (260)

The contract that McMurphy keeps is Emersonian in nature. It grows out of conscience, integrity, as Emerson explained in "Self-Reliance": "High be his heart, faithful his will, clear his sight, that he may in good earnest be doctrine, society, law, to himself, that a simple purpose may be to him as strong as iron necessity is to others!" Although it is clear that McMurphy had no intention of escaping and leaving the men to face alone the consequences of the party he had arranged, Bromden is certainly right that McMurphy did what he did because he had "signed on for the whole game." It is also clear that McMurphy knew at least from the day of the fight in the shower that the whole game would take his life, but even without him, the ward reverberates with McMurphy's spirit: "She tried to get her ward back into shape," Bromden reports, "but it was difficult with McMurphy's presence still tromping up and down the halls and laughing out loud in the meetings and singing in the latrines"(269). It is this spirit that inspires Bromden's performance of the euthanasia and his subsequent escape to extend the spirit to others.[22] The remarkable but credible rise of McMurphy from con man to hero to martyred offbeat messiah is a thematic testimony through characterization to values more important than the mere survival of an individual—values such as love, dignity, freedom, justice. As the embodiment of this truth, McMurphy transcends the caricature that initially defines him and to which as mere villain Big Nurse remains tied. Kesey pits one against the other not to show the easy victory of a credible character over a straw figure but to demonstrate through dramatic contrast by how much humanity is superior to inhumanity.

The psychological growth of Bromden is stimulated by and parallels the moral growth of McMurphy. As a six-foot-eight-inch Columbia Gorge Indian, Bromden is physically imposing though he imagines himself tiny. Several textual references call attention to his size. "Big enough to eat apples off my head," says one of the aides, "an' he mine me like a baby"(9). McMurphy tells Bromden in their

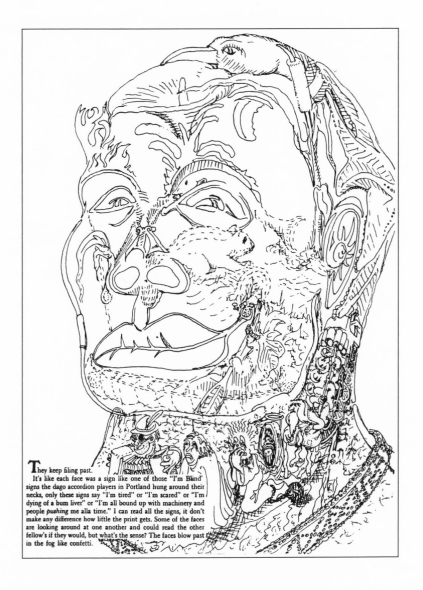

They keep filing past.

It's like each face was a sign like one of those "I'm Blind" signs the dago accordion players in Portland hung around their necks, only these signs say "I'm tired" or "I'm scared" or "I'm dying of a bum liver" or "I'm all bound up with machinery and people *pushing* me alla time." I can read all the signs, it don't make any difference how little the print gets. Some of the faces are looking around at one another and could read the other fellow's if they would, but what's the sense? The faces blow past in the fog like confetti.

first conversation, "The first thing I saw when I came in this place was you sitting over in that chair, big as a damn mountain. I tell you, I lived over Klamath and Texas and Oklahoma and all over around Gallup, and I swear you're the biggest Indian I ever saw"(186). Despite his actual size, Bromden thinks of himself after long years of attrition by the Combine as small and weak. He tells McMurphy that he cannot stand up for himself against the aides and Big Nurse: "I'm way too little. I used to be big, but not no more. You're twice the size of me"(186), yet in the swimming pool Bromden has observed that McMurphy "was having to tread water where I was just standing on the bottom"(147). Bromden's distorted sense of his own size is another manifestation of the intimidating power of the Combine, but, more important, it is evidence of the vulnerability of the human spirit. Moreover, Bromden's sense of his own physical diminution has its counterpart in his negative attitudes and defeatist views of the world.

In his account of a scene from his childhood, Bromden reveals the origin of his feeling of insignificance. The government purchasing agents who come to negotiate the acquisition of the tribal lands simply ignore Bromden as a subhuman ten-year-old irrelevancy. They talk about him and his people as though he is neither present nor sentient nor articulate. When he speaks, they do not acknowledge his speech. With his hypersensitive perception, he sees "the apparatus inside them take the words I just said and try to fit the words in here and there, this place and that, and when they find the words don't have any place ready-made where they'll fit, the machinery disposes of the words like they weren't even spoken"(181); thus, Bromden remembers, his deafness and dumbness were not originally feigned but discovered: "it wasn't me that started acting deaf; it was people that first started acting like I was too dumb to hear or see or say anything at all"(178). As Ralph Ellison's Invisible Man came to invisibility, so Bromden comes to deafness and dumbness, and this withdrawal from the world leads him to choose paranoia as a way of life in the ward: "They [the aides] don't bother not talking out loud about their hate secrets when I'm nearby because they think I'm deaf and dumb. Everybody thinks so. I'm cagey enough to fool them that much. If my being half Indian ever helped me in any way in this dirty life, it helped me being cagey, helped me all these years"(10). Bromden's caginess with Big Nurse takes the form of the avoidance of eye contact: "I let the mop push me back to the wall and smile and try to foul her equipment up as much as possible by not letting her see my eyes—they can't tell so much about you if you got your eyes closed"(10). Although his life is miserable for him, Bromden is humped protectively over it in an expression of some animalistic instinct for mere survival. This is the instinct that McMurphy must first perceive and then build on, but to do so he must penetrate Bromden's pose. He does so on their first meeting by looking into his eyes. Bromden remembers that after his first scrutiny, McMurphy "was laughing because he wasn't fooled for one minute by my deaf-and-dumb act; it didn't make any difference *how* cagey the act was, he was onto me and was laughing and winking to let me know it"(26). But Bromden is slow to respond to McMurphy, for his fear is long ingrained, and it has eroded his confidence and his philosophy.

After witnessing the humiliation and destruction of his father, after enduring the absurdities of war, and after surviving over fifteen years on the ward and, as Harding reports, "more than two hundred shock treatments"(65), Bromden views the world as bleak and hopeless, a "dirty life." He sees the ward as an unnatural habitat for manic and helpless men who are too weak to live and too scared to die. Their need for help is a silent, ubiquitous cry in the air, but Bromden believes there is no help available. In an unspoken response to Billy's need, for example, Bromden confesses, "I can't do nothing for you either, Billy. You know that. None of us can. You got to understand that as soon as a man goes to help somebody, he leaves himself wide open. He *has* to be cagey, Billy, you should know that as well as anyone"(121). Bromden observes the same self-protective strategy in McMurphy after his talk with the lifeguard. What makes things hopeless to Bromden is the power of Big Nurse and what she represents:

> She covers one whole side of the room like a Jap statue. There's no moving her and no help against her. She's lost a little battle here today [McMurphy's tub-room victory], but it's a minor battle in a big war that she's been winning and that she'll go on winning. We

mustn't let McMurphy get our hopes up any different, lure us into making some kind of dumb play. She'll go on winning, just like the Combine, because she has all the power of the Combine behind her. (101)

This kind of defeatism in his view of the ward and the world has led Bromden to philosophical despair. "And eventually," he concludes, "we all got to lose. Nobody can help that"(101). His response to these bleak prospects is characteristic of the trembling creature he has become: he withdraws.

The fog that Bromden imagines emanating from the walls of the hospital is really a psychological cloud of his own making. Whenever things get too tough or painful or confusing for Bromden to cope with, he retreats into his fog, but he tries to salvage some self-respect by attributing the fog to an external source. The historical source of this mental cloud was the fog machine Bromden saw in the army that was used to hide airplanes and men against enemy attack. In the fog, "You were safe from the enemy, but you were awfully alone"(116). One found his way out of the fog, Bromden remembers, by following a horn that, significantly, "sounded like a goose honking." The passage documents Bromden's condition in the fog as well as prefigures symbolically the direction he must take to get out of it. His long dependence on this psychological defense is, however, hard to break. On the day that McMurphy is admitted to the ward, for example, Bromden is deeply immersed in his fog:

> Before noontime they're at the fog machine again but they haven't got it turned up full; it's not so thick but what I can see if I strain real hard. One of these days I'll quit straining and let myself go completely, lose myself in the fog the way some of the other Chronics have, but for the time being I'm interested in this new man—I want to see how he takes to the Group Meeting coming up. (42)

The power of McMurphy to lure Bromden out of his fog, indicated here, or push him back into it is sustained as a pattern in the novel.

Characterization

Bromden sinks back into his fog when McMurphy loses the first TV vote, but he emerges from his fog under McMurphy's influence to provide the decisive twenty-first vote the second time around, when McMurphy wins his bet.[23] With McMurphy's withdrawal from the struggle against Big Nurse, Bromden goes back into his fog: "Whatever it was went haywire in the mechanism, they've just about got it fixed again"(156), and Bromden's narration sinks into the fog of a blank page. Although the fog is a source of temporary protection for Bromden, he knows it is also a form of nonexistence that in moments of despair he even finds attractive, as above, or in this: "Now, I don't know. Being lost isn't so bad"(118). Such an admission is an indication of the extent of his illness and a measure of the distance McMurphy has to cover to bring him back into mental health and manhood.

The mentoring of McMurphy and the growth of Bromden develop by fits and starts, but, however uneven, the movement is away from death and toward life. The process of renewal starts with the return of Bromden's senses. Involuntarily, Bromden reveals to McMurphy that he can hear: "Why, you sure did give a jump when I told you that coon was coming, Chief. I thought somebody told me you was deef"(77), and later in his response to McMurphy's gift of a pack of gum, Bromden reveals voluntarily that he can speak: "I picked up the package of gum from the bedspread and held it in my hand and told him Thank you"(185). McMurphy brings a new scent into the ward. Instead of the usual "smells of germicide, zinc ointment, and foot powder, smell of piss and sour old-man manure, of Pablum and eyewash," Bromden picks up from McMurphy a long-forgotten odor, "the man smell of dust and dirt from the open fields, and sweat, and work"(91). Under McMurphy's courage to be "what he is," and enjoy his life to the fullest, Bromden emerges from his self-imposed darkness: "I was seeing lots of things different. I figured the fog machine had broke down in the walls when they turned it up too high for that meeting on Friday, so now they weren't able to circulate fog and gas and foul up the way things looked"(140–41). All of Bromden's senses are fully awakened in the moving nighttime scene when Bromden, unmedicated, peers significantly from the darkness of the ward through a window at the moonlit natural scene beyond the walls of the hospital. He sees the stars and moon and trees and pastureland. He feels the cool breeze and the cold wire mesh against his forehead and the chilly dew on his face. He smells silage and the fall aroma of burnt leaves. He hears the shade popping and a flock of geese passing over, and he watches a young dog frolicking in the wet grass:

> . . . Galloping from one particularly interesting hole to the next, he became so took with what was coming off—the moon up there, the night, the breeze full of smells so wild makes a young dog drunk—that he had to lie down on his back and roll. . . .
>
> He sniffed all the holes over once again one quick one, to get the smells down good, then suddenly froze still with one paw lifted and his head tilted, listening. I listened too, . . . Then, from a long way off, I heard a high, laughing gabble, faint and coming closer, Canada honkers going south for the winter. I remembered all the hunting and belly-crawling I'd ever done trying to kill a honker, and that I never got one.
>
> . . . The dog could still hear them a long time after me. He was still standing with his paw up; he hadn't moved or barked when they flew over. When he couldn't hear them any more either, he commenced to lope off in the direction they had gone, toward the highway, loping steady and solemn like he had an appointment. (142–43)

The joyous physical activity of the dog in this scene matches the reawakening of Bromden's senses, and the direction he takes in pursuit of the wild geese points the way to Bromden's eventual path of escape. The honking of the geese is linked in Bromden's consciousness to the horn the army lieutenant used to blow to lead the men out of the defensive fog. Since the goose is his totem, it is appropriate that he has never killed one. The scene as a whole, then, marks the physical return of Bromden to life and sets up his liberation.

Merely to feel alive, however, is not enough. Bromden's sentient growth leads to psychological and moral growth under McMurphy's guiding hand. Although Bromden at first attributes his courage to lift his hand in the second TV vote to McMurphy's manipulation—

"McMurphy's got hidden wires hooked to it, lifting it slow just to get me out of the fog"—he concludes that the act was his own: "No. That's not the truth. I lifted it myself"(126). His independence continues on the fishing trip as he feels himself among the others, "part of them, laughing with them—and somehow not with them"(212); his optimism grows in the aftermath when he notices "I was getting so's I could see some good in the life around me"(216). His courage grows when he assists McMurphy in the shower fight, and his resolution grows afterwards when he fights off the fog following the EST treatment and declares, "It's fogging a little, but I won't slip off and hide in it. No . . . never again. . . . I saw an aide coming up the hall with a tray for me and knew this time I had them beat"(241).

This resolve sustains him in the tradition of McMurphy's "Guts ball" credo when he returns to the ward from Disturbed and has to perform the hero's role in the absence of McMurphy, sustaining the men in their continuing need for a leader. The final test of his full growth, though, occurs when McMurphy's lobotomized body is returned to the ward. There is no moral precedent in Bromden's experience for the taking of McMurphy's life, and Bromden arrives at the existential decision to do so in fear and trembling, but with complete independence—and despite the instinctual resistance of McMurphy: "The big, hard body had a tough grip on life. It fought a long time against having it taken away . . ."(270). The suffocating embrace of death is also an embrace of love, and it formalizes the passing of the torch of life from McMurphy to Bromden. A complete human being at last, and embued with the spirit of McMurphy, Bromden celebrates his transformation in his triumphant bursting forth from the cuckoo's nest and in his liberating run—"flying, Free"—in the direction of the wild geese and toward life and others who may need his help. "I been away," he declares, "a long time"(272). The dramatic development of Bromden from the sickest man in the ward to a confident, resilient hero is a masterful piece of characterization. It documents the novel's thematic contention that the best that is in man, properly nourished, can overcome the worst that is in him. Bromden is thus the central figure in the novel not only because of the scope of his development but also because of his function as narrator, as will become clear in the later discussion of point of view.

SUPPORTING CHARACTERS

As a college graduate and thus the president of the Patient's Council, Harding is designated by Billy as the "Bull Goose Loony" with whom McMurphy must conduct mock negotiations for leadership of the ward in the opening section of the novel. Harding's personal problems grow out of his homosexuality. "I indulged," he tells McMurphy, "in certain practices that our society regards as shameful. And I got sick. It wasn't the practices, I don't think, it was the feeling that the great, deadly, pointing forefinger of society was pointing at me . . ."(257). Made ashamed by the fact that he is "different" and unable to live with his shame, Harding becomes one of the Combine's discards. His voluptuous wife, Vera, seems to serve as the spokesperson for the Combine by constantly reminding him of his "difference," his effeminate ways: "Dale," she asks, "when are you going to learn to laugh instead of making that mousy little squeak?"(158) or "Oh Dale, you never do have enough, do you?"(158). Harding tries to hide his incapacities and his humiliation in erudite wit, urbane sarcasm, and oversmoking. Like W. H. Auden, Harding wishes "to put a little smoke between himself and the world" and is thus a bit like Bromden with his fog.

Bull Goose Loony or not, Harding functions as the spokesman for the ward. He provides McMurphy with the appropriate animal analogy for the inmates: "We comical little creatures can't even achieve masculinity in the rabbit world, that's how weak and inadequate we are. Hee. We are—the *rabbits*, one might say, of the rabbit world!"(63). Harding explains the rules for self-preservation to guide McMurphy in the bet over control, and he also reveals to McMurphy the startling fact on which the plot turns, that most of the men were not committed but are in the hospital voluntarily. It is to Harding, therefore, that McMurphy turns for an answer to the central question about the cause for the kind of confusion he has become enmeshed in in the hospital. "What happens?"(257), McMurphy asks simply. Harding cannot give a simple answer, but he does provide an explanation for McMurphy's sacrifice. "It is us"(258)—the weak and victimized—that drive strong men to self-destruction in the cause of brotherhood. As a beneficiary of McMurphy's real commitment, Harding sees himself going "right out that front door, with all the traditional red tape and complications. I want my wife to be here in a car at a certain time to pick me up. I want them to know I was *able* to do it that way"(257). And that is precisely how Harding does leave the hospital, but not before he has told Big Nurse to her face, in McMurphy's behalf, that she is "full of so much bullshit"(269). Harding has not changed his sexual preference—and McMurphy has never chided him about that—but he has outgrown his shame over it, and he has decided that he will not let the disapproval of society intimidate him over his difference to the extent that he will deprive himself of whatever joy he can derive from life. He leaves the hospital as another credit to the healthy influence of McMurphy.

Billy Bibbit is the boy-man on the ward, an appealing little-brother type who is a thirty-one-year-old stuttering innocent based on Melville's Billy Budd.[24] Billy's psycholinguistic handicap, a manifestation of an acute failure of self-confidence, is compounded by an egocentric, overprotective mother and by Nurse Ratched, who trades on both Billy's weakness and her friendship with Mrs. Bibbit. Bromden thinks of Billy in terms of a Norman Rockwell calendar: "like a jug-eared and freckled-faced and buck-toothed kid whistling barefoot across one of those calendars with a string of bullheads dragging behind him in the dust—"(246) and yet when Bromden actually sees him with others, he is surprised to notice "that he wasn't jug-eared or freckled or buck-toothed at all under a closer look, and was, in fact, thirty-some years old"(246). Although Billy gives the impression of inchoate youth, he is actually approaching middle age; his apparent youthfulness is a function of arrested development. In Group Meeting he confesses painfully, "The first word I said I st-stut-tered: m-m-m-m-mamma"(119), and reveals that he quit ROTC and flunked out of college because in response to roll calls he could only stammer "heh—heh—heh . . ."(119). Because of his boyish appeal and usual good nature, Billy is a special favorite of McMurphy, who is shocked by Billy's emotional response in the group conversation over the voluntary-committed matter:

> "Sure!" It's Billy, turned from the screen, his face boiling tears. "Sure!" he screams again. "If we had the g-guts! I could go outside to-today, if I had the guts. . . ."
>
> "You think I wuh-wuh-wuh-*want* to stay in here? You think I wouldn't like a con-con-vertible and a guh-guh-girl friend? But did you ever have people l-l-laughing at you? No, because you're so b-big and so *tough!* Well, I'm not big and tough. Neither is Harding. Neither is F-Fredrickson. Neither is Suh-Sefelt. Oh—oh, you—you t-talk like we stayed in here because we like it! Oh—it's no use . . ." (168)

The intensity of this verbal explosion is an epiphany to McMurphy of the depth of Billy's hurt and need—and by extension of the pain and needs of the others—and it compels him to end his withdrawal and take up their cause with greater conviction. Billy's tears come from the boy in him, his anguish from the man he wishes to be.

Despite McMurphy's friendship, encouragement, dancing lessons, and sexual therapy with Candy, Billy, like Billy Budd, is doomed, and he telegraphs his suicide in several ways. His participation in the attack on Harding in Group Meeting leads him to self-disgust and an embarrassed confession of weakness to McMurphy: "Ah, It's n-no use. I should just k-k-kill myself"(64). He has cigarette burns on the backs of his hands from torturing himself and razor-blade scars on his wrists from previous attempts at suicide (121), and his only love affair ended in humiliation: "And even when I pr-proposed, I flubbed it. I said 'Huh-honey, will you muh-muh-muh-muh-muh . . .' til the girl broke out l-laughing"(121). Under McMurphy's tutelage, Billy makes some progress toward manhood—on the fishing trip and in the "nuptial" night with Candy—but he cannot sustain that growth under the maternal shaming of Big Nurse when she discovers him in bed with a prostitute. "What worries me, Billy," Big Nurse clucks slyly, "is how your poor mother is going to take this"(264). With his temporary manhood thus deflated, Billy reverts immediately to a boyish strategy of shifting responsibility to others, to Candy and McMurphy and the inmates, and then in Dr. Spivey's office he cuts his throat and ends his life in abject shame in an actual performance of the act that he has threatened for most of his adult life. The enormity of this senseless and unnecessary tragedy drives McMurphy, Billy's "special friend and hero"(221), to commit in retaliation his ultimate attack on Big Nurse. Billy's death documents the tremendous power and danger of the Combine, and it triggers the resolution of the plot.

Another little man trying to grow bigger—and also doomed—is Cheswick. According to Bromden, Cheswick is "one of these guys who'll make a big fuss like he's going to lead an attack, holler charge and stomp up and down a minute, take a couple steps, and quit"(62). Because Cheswick sees McMurphy as the embodiment of the hero he himself would like to be, he imitates McMurphy and feeds on McMurphy's strength: "He's pleased to be sitting next to McMurphy, feeling brave like this. It's the first time Cheswick ever had somebody along with him on his lost causes"(105). Cheswick's dependency on McMurphy is excessive, however, for when McMurphy, during his withdrawal, fails to back up Cheswick in the cigarette debate, the little hero manqué cannot survive the blow to his fragile ego. Although Cheswick tells McMurphy he understands the self-protective defection, he cannot live with its consequences for his future. The most heroic act of his life is the deliberate taking of it in the very pool where McMurphy learned to guard his own life, an act that points up again the force of the Combine and the terrible need of the men that draws McMurphy back into the risky fray.

Martini, the grand hallucinator, functions in the ward as both fool and "seer." His tenuous contact with reality is usually a source of entertainment for the other inmates. In the monopoly game, for example, though his token is in his mouth, he hallucinates his "things" all over the board, but McMurphy stills all complaints about Martini's mode of play: "Cheswick, you never mind about Martini. He's doing real good. . . . ; don't we get rent from him every time one of his 'things' lands on our property?"(102). And when Martini confronts the chest x-ray machine, he comes away astounded: "I wouldn't of believed it if I hadn't saw it"(167). Martini also teaches the service station attendants the difference between a bug stain and a bird stain on the windshield: "There'd be feathers and bones if it was a bird"(202). Just as often, however, Martini's visions are serious. In his imaginary dogfight with enemy aircraft in the tub room, Martini suddenly conjures up in the shower stall the ghosts of desperate need past and present, and in his role as seer urges McMurphy's attention: "Hold it a minute," Martini implores McMurphy, "They need you to see thum"(161). Martini's extrasensory perception is both comic and profound. His character seems at a metaphysical level to grow out of Bromden's question about the horrible events he himself imagines in the hospital—"But if they don't exist, how can a man see them?"(82)—and at a practical level, Martini's character is a partial gloss on Bromden's cryptic assertion early in the novel that "it's the truth even if it didn't happen"(13). That is, reality in the ward as it is experienced psychically is far more complex than the sum of its empirically verifiable parts.

Other characters serve, for the most part, as what Henry James called "*ficelles*," functionaries who provide verisimilitude, advance the plot, or contrast sharply with more fully developed characters.

Most of the Chronics and many of the Acutes, for example, document in simple but vivid ways both their own wretchedness and the range of grotesque shapes thrown off in the chaff from the Combine. Pete Bancini, whose lifetime exertions to overcome his mental handicap have left him exhausted, can only state his condition in pure veracity: "Oh, I'm *awful* tired . . ."(42). Ellis, the Acute who was rendered a Chronic by careless Electro-Shock Therapy, stands with hands outstretched in mute crucifixion against the wall of the institution that destroyed his brain. By the same process, Ruckly has been reduced to a retarded vaudeville figure with a single sad-silly one-liner response to every stimulus: "Fffffffuck da wife!"(21). The old cavalryman, Colonel Matterson, patiently teaches from "the wrinkled scripture of that long yellow hand" the strange but compelling analogies that he has derived from his combative life: "The flag is . . . Ah-mer-ica. America is . . . the plum. The peach. The wah-ter-mel-on. . . . Now . . . The cross is . . . Mex-i-co"(120). Sefelt and Fredrickson with their epilepsy and destructive dependency on Dilantin demonstrate the truth of Scanlon's observation: "Hell of a life," Scanlon observes, "Damned if you do and damned if you don't. Puts a man in one confounded *bind,* I'd say"(155). Rawler the Squawler in Disturbed expresses his sense of the bind he is in with an eerie, inarticulate howl—"Looooo, looo"—and ends his anguish by castrating himself and bleeding to death into the toilet bowl. In every instance, these figures establish in haunting verisimilitude that life is hard and man is vulnerable.

Other characters, whose sympathies are more outside than inside the ward, function as contrasting or conflicting figures. Public Relation is in fact named by his function. When he guides visitors through the hospital, women schoolteachers for example, he bubbles with goodwill: "What a *cheery* atmosphere, don't you agree? . . . Oh, when I think back on the old days, on the filth, the bad food, even, yes, brutality, oh, I realize, ladies, that we have come a long way in our campaign!"(14) and, as Bromden notes, "he's laughing most of the time I don't ever know what at, laughing high and fast like he wishes he could stop but can't do it"(37). His laughter is, transparently, semihysteria created by the disparity between the appearances he tries to peddle and the stark reality that belies them. Dr. Spivey is also more an outsider than an insider. Shy, weak, able to be intimidated, he is first the puppet of Big Nurse and then of McMurphy, who learns quickly that the doctor can be manipulated to change ward policy, acquire a game room, approve a fishing trip, and in general loosen the grip of taut control the Big Nurse exercises over the ward. The staring commuters on the highway, the bullying attendants at the service station, and the wise-guy kibitzers on the dock are mere stick figures whose simple role is to advance the rise or decline of the central characters by providing opposition. They are neither personalized nor developed.

Although Kesey depends heavily on caricature in this novel, he seems to find it difficult not to personalize his characters. Harding, Billy, Cheswick, and Martini certainly come alive and cast a shadow, and even the very minor supporting characters are often endowed with features that make their cameo appearances memorable. Colonel Matterson, the oldest man on the ward, will sometimes interrupt his history lessons because he "is given to lifting the skirts of passing nurses with his cane"(21). Sefelt is memorable when he introduces Sandy to epileptic intercourse. She certainly thinks so: "Never in my life experienced anything to come even *halfway* near it"(255). And, perhaps inspired by the growth of the others on the fishing trip, Dr. Spivey shows considerable spunk in battling for several hours and landing an enormous fish (a flounder, George says; a halibut, says a man on the dock). Of those who are able to leave the ward as a result of McMurphy's influence, they leave transformed from caricatures. Harding, the spokesman, pronounces the change: "They're still sick men in lots of ways. But at least there's that: they are sick *men* now. No more rabbits, Mack. Maybe they can be well men someday"(257).

The minor female characters in the novel, however, fall rather easily into two categories, good women and bad women. The women so designated are sometimes humanized to a small extent, but for the most part they remain caricatures. One good woman is the Japanese nurse on the Disturbed ward who sympathizes with Bromden and McMurphy, binds their wounds tenderly, and assures them "It's not all like her [Big Nurse's] ward"(234). Two other "good" women are, ironically, the strippers and hookers Candy and Sandy. Unlike Nurse Ratched, they are not ashamed of their womanhood or embarrassed by eroticism, they like men, and they share McMurphy's joie de vivre. Both of them have an appealing gusto, but they are still mindless stereotypes in the tradition of the whore with the heart of gold, as the Japanese woman is cast in the mold of the compassionate nurse.

The bad women in the novel seem to be variations on the type represented by Big Nurse—emasculating women, or "ball cutters" as McMurphy has it. They are aggressive, manipulative women who have traded their nurturing female natures for power or control. The government woman who comes to purchase the tribal lands of Bromden's people, for instance, urges her male counterparts to be cagey and circumvent the chief, to "type up an offer—and mail it to the wife, you see, by mistake? I feel our job will be a great deal easier" for "As my sociology professor used to emphasize, 'There is generally one person in every situation you must never underestimate the power of' "(182). She is one of the manipulative women, as is Mrs. Bromden, a one-hundred-and thirty-pound woman whom her son remembers as "Bigger than Papa and me together"(186) and as an accomplice to the Combine in the fatal reduction of Tee Ah Millatoona: "Oh the Combine's big—big. He fought it a long time till my mother made him too little to fight any more and he gave up"(187). Mrs. Bibbit deliberately treats her thirty-one-year-old Billy as a little boy in order to feed her vanity and perpetuate illusions of her own youth: "*Sweet*heart, do I look like the mother of a middle-aged man?"(247). And Vera Harding flaunts her sexuality as an exercise in power and as an indictment of her husband's effeminacy, which she both deplores and exploits: "She says any man that drops around to see her flips more than his damned wrists"(159). As types, these women are merely functionaries; they serve to show, either in causality or complicity, the powers of distortion intrinsic to the Combine and to those affected by it. The opposition of gender in this conflict of characters does not favor either side: the excessive power or malice of the women is matched by the excessive weakness or ineptitude of the men. That is, if the male perception as represented by Harding—"We are victims of a matriarchy here"(59)—is set over against the female perception as represented by Big Nurse—"He is simply a man and no more, and is subject to all the fears and all the cowardice and all the timidity that any other man is subject to"(136)—the two contrasting opinions add up in the overall strategy of the novel not to a sexual problem, but to a human problem. Kesey employs the sexual conflict in the novel as a device to argue against the kind of internecine warfare that McMurphy decries after witnessing the general battles between Big Nurse and the men and the particular one between Vera and Dale Harding. "Hell's bells, Harding!," McMurphy exclaims, ". . . All I know is this: nobody's very big in the first place, and it looks to me like everybody spends their whole life tearing everybody else down"(159). From McMurphy and for the novel, this cautionary criticism cuts across gender lines.

The issue of ostensible sexism in the novel has generated a good deal of critical comment, from the borderline hysteria of Marcia Falk's letter to the editor of the *New York Times* (cited earlier) to more carefully reasoned analyses by critics male and female.[25] Ron Billingsley has rightly argued, I think, that "it would be a serious mistake to read the novel as the work of a misogynist. Big Nurse and her emasculating ilk are no more truly feminine than the Acutes and Dr. Spivey are truly masculine. Like machines, these women are neuter, asexual devices that respond to *power*."[26] Stephen Tanner writes persuasively to the same point: "Miss Ratched is a villain not because she is a woman, but because she is not human. McMurphy's ripping open of her shell-like uniform is not a revengeful attack on a castrating bitch: It is a symbolic gesture indicating that the human must be liberated from the machine if the oppression of the Combine is to be eliminated."[27] Kesey uses sexual conflict for dramatic focus on the more encompassing matter of human distortions and vulnerabilities. To see the novel only in terms of gender is to mistake the medium for the message. To state the matter another way, it is always possible to find a rat turd in a silo, but it is a lot of trouble, that is not what the silo is built for, and the discovery is hardly worth the effort.

7

SYMBOLISM

As the nocturnal revelry during the wild party on the ward approaches crescendo—madder music, stronger wine, wheelchair tag, and epileptic sex—Harding offers a caption for the scene: "It isn't happening. It's all a collaboration of Kafka and Mark Twain and Martini"(254). The mode that Harding describes is a combination of realism and symbolism with a bit of twentieth-century hallucinogenics thrown in for color. Kesey's realism grows naturally out of his regionalism:

> Kesey, perhaps more than any contemporary American writer, has the touch of actuality—of a landscape that has been seen, a dialogue which has been heard, an action which in spite of its heroic qualities is to be believed. He knows how the *outside* looks to one who is fettered *inside;* he knows not only how the rainsoaked forest of coastal Oregon looks, he knows how it feels to endure whole seasons of rain. He knows the language of the working people about whom he writes; he is one of the few writers who can set down the incessantly obscene talk of the working stiff without sounding as though he's done it to offend.[28]

Kesey himself has commented on the realistic/regionalistic dimension of his fiction: "Yes, I work out of where my feet fit the ground." He emphasizes his role as storyteller in an ancient form; he wants to get his stories "off the page and back in front of people, back by the camp-fire. I'm interested only in the magic of storytelling."[29] Although Kesey describes himself here as a teller of tales in a realistic oral tradition reminiscent of Twain, he allows for the admixture of Kafkasque symbolism in his use of the phrase "the magic of storytelling." His presentational mode, then, includes "the meal in the firkin, the milk in the pan" as well as the genie in the lamp and "Lucy in the Sky with Diamonds." In the skillful blending of realistic forms with symbolic resonance, *Cuckoo's Nest* ranges freely through elements of popular culture, folklore, mythology, and Christianity.

POPULAR CULTURE

Popular culture supplies the materials for much of Kesey's symbolism. The conflict of opposing visions that Henry Adams characterized as the Virgin versus the Dynamo and Leo Marx has seen as the Machine versus the Garden[30] appears in the high-tech culture depicted in *Cuckoo's Nest* as a continuing man/machine opposition in the contrasts between Bromden's mechanistic imagery (gears, cogs, wheels, tubes, wires, Nurse "Ratched," the Combine) and his natural imagery (birds, animals, water, sky, landscapes). Most damaging of all, the human form has been invaded by the machine. In Bromden's vision of the eviseration of Blastic, no human organs emerge but "just a shower of rust and ashes, and now and again a piece of wire or glass"(81), and Bromden finds it easy to toss Warren into the shower because "He was full of tubes; he didn't weigh more'n ten or fifteen pounds"(231). Big Nurse carries a wicker bag "full of a thousand parts she aims to use in her duties today—wheels and gears, cogs polished to a hard glitter, tiny pills that gleam like porcelain, needles, forceps, watch-makers' pliers, rolls of copper wire . . ."(10) to keep her people in good repair. Against this dehumanizing death force must come a rehuman-izing life force: McMurphy, in his black shorts with the white whales

on them, is the virile life giver born into popular culture out of liter-
ature by way of an Oregon State co-ed who had read enough of *Moby
Dick* to know he was a sperm whale and thus to give the shorts to
McMurphy because he "was a symbol"(76). One of the residents also
knows enough nineteenth-century American literature to classify
McMurphy according to a popular Thoreauvian formulation:
"You know, like 'He Who Marches Out of Step Hears Another
Drum' "(133). The life-giver and stepper-to-another-drum teaches that
nature is superior to the machine and shows how the fearful social
engine can be sabotaged from within in the human use of the symbolic
control panel to shatter control.

Popular culture also supplies the music that Kesey employs as
significant leitmotifs in the novel. McMurphy dislikes the Muzak-style
tape that plays incessantly in the day room because its characterless
homogeneity is for him emblematic of what the ward tries to do to
people. McMurphy himself, though, uses music to good effect in his
relations with others. On his first morning in the hospital, McMurphy
is heard in the latrine singing several verses of "The Wagoner's Lad":
" 'My horses ain't hungry, they won't eat your hay-ay-aeee.' He holds
the note and plays with it, then swoops down with the rest of the verse
to finish it off. 'So fare-thee-well, darlin', I'm gone on my way' "(83),
and "Hard livin's my pleasure, my money's my o-o-own, an' them that
don't like me, they can leave me alone"(87). In this scene, he sings to
express his animal good spirits, but the verses of the song also express
his disdain for place. Later in the hall, as Washington sidles toward
an angry Big Nurse, McMurphy whistles, with ironic allusion to the
Globetrotters, "Sweet Georgia Brown" as comic accompaniment to
the aide's evasive shuffle. After shocking Nurse Ratched with his
whale shorts, he accompanies her hasty retreat to the Nurses' Station
with a bit of verse from "The Roving Gambler" (a song he started in
the admission scene) to establish his style, define his character, and
show his indifference to policy: " 'She took me to her parlor, and coo-
oo-ooled me with her fan'—I can hear the whack as he slaps his bare
belly—'whispered low in her mamma's ear, I luh-uhvvv that gamblin'
man' "(91). As a way of breaking the ice with Bromden on the night

the Chief reveals that he can talk, McMurphy sings him a silly hillbilly song: " 'Oh, does the Spearmint lose its flavor on the bedpost overnight?' "(184). These musical signs are painted with a light touch, but they add dimension to both character and scene.

More important than popular literary formulations or musical motifs, however, are references to television and the movies. Harding characterizes the inmates as harmless animations "Hippity-hopping through our Walt Disney world" (61), and into this world comes McMurphy to challenge the wicked witch. "He walked with long steps, too long, and he had his thumbs hooked in his pockets again. The iron in his boot heels cracked lightning out of the tile. He was the logger again, the swaggering gambler, the big redheaded brawling Irishman, the cowboy out of the TV set walking down the middle of the street to meet a dare"(172). When McMurphy is taken to the Disturbed ward after the fight in the shower, he reenacts for a new audience his original entry into the hospital, and he does so in deliberate histrionic exaggeration: " 'McMurphy's the name, pardners,' he said in his drawling cowboy actor's voice, 'an' the thing I want to *know* is who's the peckerwood runs the poker game in this establishment' "(232). McMurphy sustains this movie-hero bravado all the way to the end, when, "like one of those moving-picture zombies, obeying orders beamed at him from forty masters," he attacks Big Nurse physically in the obligatory showdown between hero and villain: "We made him stand and hitch up his black shorts like they were horsehide chaps, and push back his cap with one finger like it was a ten-gallon Stetson, slow, mechanical gestures—and when he walked across the floor you could hear the iron in his bare heels ring sparks out of the tile"(267). The role that McMurphy carries out is the symbolic embodiment of the "guts ball" champion's creed that he has inherited from cinema and television, and he sustains the role from beginning to end. At the beginning, his acting is playful caricature, but by the end, it becomes clear that he is playing the role at enormous personal cost. He teaches lessons in heroism as he himself is in the process of learning them, and thus he grows personally to fit the superhuman dimensions of the role he has cast himself in. His life comes to imitate art, but to imitate it so well that only his death can serve as a reminder that he is human and vulnerable after all—and thus even more admirable.

This delicate balance between caricature and character is equally evident in the cartoon motif. Bromden indicates early that the ward is "Like a cartoon world, where the figures are flat and outlined in black, jerking through some kind of goofy story that might be real funny if it weren't for the cartoon figures being real guys . . ."(34). Technicians in the hospital speak with voices that "are forced and too quick on the comeback to be real talk—more like cartoon comedy speech"(36), and under Big Nurse's watchful eye, "the scene before her takes on that blue-steel clarity again, that clean orderly movement of a cartoon comedy"(37). Bromden delineates a risky rhetorical strategy here: the attempt to render genuine human pain in a form usually limited to simplistic didacticism or comedy. Kesey's willingness to take the risk grows out of his longtime personal interest in comics and his belief that they convey truth in a special way. Kesey told Gordon Lish, for example, that "A single *Batman* comicbook is more honest than a whole volume of *Time* magazines" and that he likes to read comicbooks "because of their honest, open-handed bullshit."[31] In order to capture the true tragicomic nature of human experience, Kesey chose to render some of his characters as symbolic caricatures, others as stock figures who outgrow their black outlines. Thus Big Nurse remains a cartoon villain, comic in her excessive bluster, hateful in her manipulations and vindictiveness. She is never a sympathetic figure because she is never humanized. McMurphy, by contrast, moves from caricature to credible and then admirable human form. His status as stock western hero and defender of the weak culminates at the end of the ward party in Harding's equation of him with the Lone Ranger triumphant over injustice again, riding off into the sunset: "I'd like to stand there at the window with a silver bullet in my hand and ask 'Who *wawz* that'er masked man?' "(258). The Lone Ranger, as radio/screen/comic strip star, combines the media influences to which McMurphy is responsive. McMurphy's humanity emerges in his heroic growth to selflessness and in his instinctive struggle against death. It is sad that McMurphy must die; it is tragic and moving that his friend must take his life to prevent Big Nurse from using his mindless body as a symbol for the Combine's power. In the emotion and meaning connected with his growth and death, the caricature of McMurphy is humanized and then spiritualized.[32]

FOLKLORE

Kesey also draws on folklore to give his characterizations resonance. Although McMurphy grows into the model of frontier hero, he begins as a hell-raiser prone to disorderly conduct and "hassles." This element is suggested in his motorcycle clothes, with their symbolic connotations from urban folklore of Hell's Angels (Kesey's "friends" at one stage of his life), of wandering pariahs, and general rowdiness. The "aces and eights"(77) tattooed on one shoulder constitute, according to western folklore, the "deadman's hand" because Wild Bill Hickok was holding that hand when he was shot fatally in the back. The tattoo thus symbolizes McMurphy's cowboy character, his dangerous gamble, and his imminent death. The "Fighting Leathernecks" tattoo on the other shoulder alludes in military lore to the uniform and toughness of early U.S. Marines and thus indicates McMurphy's fighting spirit, although he says (93) that he was in the army stationed at Fort Riley, Kansas (Kesey apparently allowed folklore to take precedence over fact here, or he forgot when he gave McMurphy a Marine tattoo that McMurphy already had an Army ID). Even though Chief Bromden has an active interior life, his external appearance and behavior suggest the misfit of sociological lore, the relic from the reservation. Standing mute and sad-faced in the ward, he is a kind of cigar-store Indian or faded totem pole, a melancholy reminder of the Vanishing American. In his growing companionship with McMurphy, however, Bromden also functions in the tradition of literary lore, as Leslie Fiedler has shown, as Chingachgook, Queequeg, Jim, and Tonto to McMurphy's Natty Bumppo, Ishmael, Huck, and Lone Ranger, respectively.

Bromden is also the vehicle for a good deal of folkloric rhyming and allusion in the novel. As he endures his last Electro Shock Treatment, for instance, Bromden remembers, in rhyme, a hunt with his father (capitalization and versification added):

> Hit at a lope,
> Running already down the slope.
> Can't get back, can't go ahead,
> Look down the barrel an' you dead dead dead. (238)

And Bromden recalls in the same sequence that his father told him, "When I die, pin me up against the sky"(239). The impulse to rhyme is an impulse to order, and this manifestation of Bromden's growth in sensibility culminates in the comradeship after the fishing trip during the visit to McMurphy's homeplace. In this scene, Bromden monitors contentedly the changes he is experiencing within as a result of his exposure to McMurphy and his love for life. "McMurphy was teaching me. I was feeling better than I'd remembered feeling since I was a kid, when everything was good and the land was still singing kids' poetry to me" (216). What follows then are two remarkable pages of rhyming prose that Malcolm Cowley apparently discovered while the book was in progress and that Kesey later deliberately extended.[33] Arranged as a poem, the last few lines of Bromden's rhyming account of McMurphy's personal history with nine-year-old Judy reads as follows:

> "So my colors were flown, and from that day to this
> It seemed I might as well live up to my name—
> Dedicated lover—and it's the God's truth:
> That little nine-year-old kid out of my youth's
> The one who's to blame."
> The house drifted past.

He yawned and winked
"Taught me to love,
Bless her sweet ass." (218)

The lines are hypermetric in the passage, but the abundance of rhymes, however irregular, justifies Bromden's modest claim that what the land was singing to him was "kids' poetry." The poem emphasizes two major points—that McMurphy's role as "dedicated lover" was assigned to him at an early age and that Bromden's increasing tendency to express himself in rhyme is symbolic of his growth toward mental wholeness. He displays rhyme on his way to reason.[34]

Bromden's rhymes also give the novel its title. Rhyming has been part of Bromden's consciousness since childhood and thus part of his subconscious word selection as an adult. He remembers a rhyming game he used to play with his grandmother (versification and capitalization again added):

Tingle, tingle, tremble toes,
She's a good fisherman,
Catches hens,
Puts 'em inna pens . . .
Wire blier, limber lock,
Three geese inna flock . . .
One flew east, one flew west,
One flew over the cuckoo's nest. (239)

Bromden disliked Mrs. Tangle Toes, who put free creatures in pens, but he liked the rhyming game, he loved his grandmother, and he was especially fond of "that goose flying over the cuckoo's nest"(239). As the bird that points the way out of the cuckoo's nest, the goose, majestic in the sky, is the central symbol for freedom in the novel, even though it originates in a child's rhyming game (the American oral tradition is full of variations on this jump-rope rhyme). An important progression is signified here, too, in the accretion of traditional bird images, from the "chickens at a pecking party" in the first Group

Meeting presided over by the "old buzzard" Big Nurse (66) to the inmates as "fighting roosters" at the service station (202) to the lead goose, "bigger than the others," that engages Bromden's rapt attention as he flies across the moon and then pulls "his V out of sight into the sky once more"(143) in a demonstration to Bromden of the direction to a new life.

MYTHOLOGY

Kesey's text also resonates with the deep cello tones of mythology. With her tightly bound breasts and her practice of forming destructive dependency relationships with her charges, Big Nurse is a "terrible mother" figure of Jungian lore, as are Mrs. Bibbit and Mrs. Bromden in less dramatic forms. Charles A. Reich, in the *Greening of America,* has seen the book as a myth about "the American working man, deprived of his virility, his manhood, and his intellect by the system." The novel has also been read, as noted earlier, in terms of the Grail legend and vegetation myths. The mental ward is the waste land. Nurse Ratched as Madame Sosostris represents the waste land elements of mechanization, heartless efficiency, fear, guilt, hopelessness, and sterility, and she uses these qualities in the prolonged stultification of the inmates. McMurphy as Grail Knight enters the waste land, conquers Big Nurse at least temporarily, cures Bromden, the ailing Fisher King, and restores life to the waste land by giving the men confidence, laughter, love, and self-respect. After the mad party in the "upside-down world of the Chapel Perilous," and after the sacrificial death of McMurphy, Bromden breaks out of the waste land: "The Fisher King is free. Although the waste land remains, McMurphy the redheaded Grail Knight has symbolically transcended it through his gesture of sacrifice, and at least allowed others to 'Come in under the shadow of this red rock.' "[35]

McMurphy's heroism also follows in the pattern of what Joseph Campbell has called, in language borrowed from James Joyce, the "monomyth." The progress of the hero, according to the monomyth, is marked in formulaic but flexible rites of passage designated as "*separation-initiation-return*": "*A hero ventures forth from the world of common day,*" writes Campbell, "*into a region of supernatural wonder: fabulous forces are there encountered and a decisive victory is won: the hero comes back from this mysterious adventure with the power to bestow boons on his fellow man.*"[36] McMurphy separates himself from common manual labor on the Pendleton Work Farm to enter the fabulous world of the mental institution. There he is initiated into the wonders of pharmaceutical and mechanical mind control and the dangers of overweening matriarchal power. He accepts the challenges posed by the world he has entered—the power of Big Nurse, the weakness of the men—then withdraws from the challenges in fear and self-interest (following the lifeguard scene) but soon returns. He endures mental and physical tests (the fight with Washington, the EST treatments), wins decisive victories (the TV rebellion, the tub room, the fishing trip), and bestows boons on his followers (laughter, women, the ward party, manhood, freedom). Finally, he pays for his heroism with his life. "If the hero, instead of submitting to all of the initiatory tests, has, like Prometheus, simply darted to his goal (by violence, quick device, or luck) and plucked the boon for the world that he intended, then the powers that he has unbalanced may react so sharply that he will be blasted from within and without—crucified, like Prometheus on the rock of his own violated unconscious."[37]

McMurphy's temporary withdrawal from the adventure is what Campbell designates the "refusal of the call," and it is common for the refusal to be motivated by self-interest. "The myths and folk tales of the whole world make clear that the refusal is essentially a refusal to give up what one takes to be one's own interest."[38] When McMurphy's motivation changes from self-interest to the salvation of others, he grows to the performance of heroic actions both physical and moral and thus to the power to bestow boons on others. "The effect of the successful adventure of the hero is the unlocking and release again of the flow of life into the body of the world. The miracle of this flow may be represented in physical terms as a circulation of food substance, dynamically as a streaming of energy, or spiritually as a manifestation of grace."[39] The food substance that McMurphy provides is, of course, fish during the bountiful harvest on the sea (Doc's fish is described as the biggest halibut ever "brought in on the Oregon coast"), the energy that streams from McMurphy is captured in the significance of the initials of his name and his energizing effect on others, particularly on Bromden, and the manifestation of grace is the spiritual legacy McMurphy leaves behind to inspire the survivors to carry on and keep the faith. The transformation of such a hero involves the recognition in himself of the seeds of a higher life and a bold nurturing of these seeds into transcendent apotheosis:

> The godly powers sought and dangerously won are revealed to have been within the heart of the hero all the time. He is "the king's son" who has come to know who he is and therewith has entered into the exercise of his proper power—"God's son," who has learned to know how much that title means. From this point of view the hero is symbolical of that divine creative and redemptive image which is hidden within us all, only waiting to be known and rendered into life.[40]

Bromden expressed the concept more simply in his notion that "McMurphy was a giant come out of the sky to save us from the Combine that was networking the land with copper wire and crystal"(224).

CHRISTIANITY

McMurphy's status as "God's son" with his messianic relationship to the men in the ward is carried pointedly in the novel in extensive Christian reference and symbolism. McMurphy himself introduces the notion when he chides the men for thinking of him as "some kind of savior"(166). Despite her intentions, Big Nurse encourages thinking along these lines when she asks if any of the men could seriously consider McMurphy "a martyr or saint"(232). Both of McMurphy's hands are torn and bloodied in the tub room. On the fishing trip,

McMurphy triumphantly leads like disciples "the twelve of us toward the ocean"(203) and functions there as the "fisher of men" that Ellis had called for(199). Since the biblical miracle of the loaves and fishes, the fish has been a central Christian symbol. Prior to his punitive Electro Shock treatments, McMurphy is sent to Disturbed, where a bony Pilate figure walks around saying, "I wash my hands of the whole deal"(232). Harding describes the process of Electro Shock Therapy with explicit Christian reference: "You are strapped to a table shaped, ironically, like a cross, with a crown of electric sparks in place of thorns" (64–65). Ahead of McMurphy in line for EST is a crying man who says "It's my cross, thank you Lord, it's all I got, thank you Lord . . ."(236). As McMurphy mounts the machine for his Electro Shock crucifixion, he "spreads his arms out to fit the shadow" and asks the technicians, "Anointest my head with conductant. Do I get a crown of thorns?"(237). The charge that sears McMurphy's brain kills the sparrows on the electric lines outside the hospital: "And out the window the sparrows drop smoking off the wire"(238), an allusion to the New Testament reassurance (Matthew 10:29) that no sparrow falls without God's knowledge. The final party on the ward is a kind of Last Supper. McMurphy is the Host; Harding functions as a priest: ". . . Harding came back with a double handfull of pills; he sprinkled them over Sefelt and the woman like he was crumbling clods into a grave. He raised his eyes toward the ceiling. 'Most Merciful God, accept these two poor sinners into your arms. And keep the doors ajar for the coming of the rest of us' "(254). The sexual double-entendre of Harding's prayer accents the blending in the episode of the sacred with the profane. According to Saint John (19:30), the last words of Christ at His crucifixion were "It is finished." Bromden pronounces these words at the death of McMurphy in the form of a question: "Is it finished?"(271), to which Scanlon, also mixing the sacred and profane, replies with the expletive "Christ."

Two other symbolic scenes taken together provide a necessary gloss on McMurphy's death and Bromden's liberation. The flock of geese that Bromden sees in the night sky from the hospital window follows the biggest goose, whose flight is described as "a black cross opening and closing"(143). The young dog who is also watching the geese follows them toward the highway, and Bromden watches "the dog and the car making for the same spot of pavement." When Bromden makes his escape, he moves in the direction of the geese and the dog. In Kesey's working notes for *Cuckoo's Nest,* this passage appears in longhand:

> See that big goose up there against the moon—alone—wings spread out in a black cross.
> This means McMurphy is a wild goose. Dwell on the beauty of wild geese the magisty [sic]. Get some good visions of Canadian Honkers booming down the Columbia Gorge.[41]

Kesey's original impulse was, apparently, the simple equation of the goose with McMurphy. When impulse became art, however, the symbol took on greater complexity:

> McMurphy, "bigger than the others," wild and free and migratory is like the lead goose, pulling his followers in the direction he has chosen. . . . The symbol cluster of goose and dog is, however, a complex one, in which Bromden is ultimately associated with the goose and McMurphy with the dog. Insofar as he grows "bigger," takes over McMurphy's leadership role, and ultimately flies from the "cuckoo's nest"—"I felt like I was flying. Free."—Bromden assumes the strengths of the Canada Honker. His ultimate destination is Canada.
> Perhaps the most poignant aspect of this pattern is the foreshadowing of McMurphy's fate by that of the dog. The last glimpse Bromden has of the dog . . . shows the animal heading toward the highway . . . the "dog and the car making for the same spot of pavement." Later, when McMurphy is about to make the difficult decision to escalate his rebellion against Big Nurse, he is compared to a dog overcoming his fear of a dangerous adversary; and just before McMurphy announces his decision by breaking the window of the nurses' station, Bromden hears a sound in his head "like tires speeding down a pavement." The implicit parallel is clear: McMurphy and the dog, vital and vulnerable, move inexorably toward their head-on collisions with massive machines—the Combine and the car.[42]

The interpretation offered here demonstrates deftly the shifting intra-referentiality of the symbolism and argues persuasively for a pessimistic conclusion for the dog and McMurphy. Another critic finds the symbol cluster of goose, black cross, and dog inconclusive and unsatisfying: "The ending leaves the reader frustrated, entangled in the polarities of rebirth and destruction, freedom and oppression, hope and despair."[43] A third view, more simply negative, is that the dog's destination combined with the black cross as death symbol and the fact that the hat of the hero does not fit Bromden foreshadow by extrapolation the destruction of Bromden by the Outside Combine just as McMurphy has been destroyed by the Inside Combine. Thus "in the context of all this information, the novel's entire meaning becomes twisted if Chief's 'escape' is interpreted optimistically."[44]

Bromden does not see the dog reach the highway, however, and the reader does not see Bromden engage the Combine at the tribal falls. Informed speculation on the outcome in both cases may rest, therefore, on another scene and another symbol. As he recovers from his last Electro Shock treatment, Bromden imagines himself inside dice showing "snake eyes"—the throw in a dice game that eliminates the crapshooter trying to make his point—but he is not intimidated by the sign. "I thought the room was a dice. The number one, the snake eye up there, the circle, the white *light* in the ceiling . . . in this little room. . . . It's fogging a little, but I won't slip off and hide in it. No . . . never again . . ."(241). The image of the dice showing the snake eye suggests both the loaded dice of Fortune and the serpentine Christian symbol for Evil, but Bromden is not frightened by either. This time he knows "he had them beat." McMurphy's model certainly serves Bromden here, too, for the swaggering gambler plays life's game without caution despite the "aces and eights" of the "deadman's hand" tattooed on his shoulder. The critical views cited above indicate that negative interpretations of McMurphy's death and Bromden's prospects are certainly possible, but the iconography of the novel and its celebrative tone compel me to a positive reading. Like the dog and geese, Bromden at the end is heading for freedom and life—and both involve risks. He has acknowledged the dangers in his use of the "loaded dice" and "snake eyes" images, and he has grown through all the evidence for negation to choose affirmation, as McMurphy grew to choose commitment to others over protection of self. Of all those who escape the cuckoo's nest under McMurphy's influence, Bromden is the least likely to be naive. He knows he will be at risk, and he will certainly die, but he will confront both eventualities on his own fighting terms. That is the heroic stature he has risen to from the pitiful husk of a man he was when McMurphy reached out to him the first day on the ward. The "black cross" may be a symbol for death, but it is also more significantly in terms of McMurphy's martyrdom a symbol for the power of sacrificial love—an acknowledgement that life is informed by values more important than mere survival.

These Christian parallels and echoes function ambivalently in the novel. They carry with them through most of the story an almost light-hearted tone, as though Kesey is indulging himself in a form of meta-fictional play with the American novel's penchant for Christ figures.[45] But McMurphy's death and transfiguration are presented in a context of high seriousness and deep emotion, as though McMurphy's growth from caricature to character, from functionary to full humanity, demands an accompanying modulation in tone from playful to reverential. It is appropriate, too, that Bromden should preside at McMurphy's death and be the one most moved by it, for in the transformation of McMurphy from the self-love of a con man to the brotherly love of a messianic martyr, Bromden has been the primary beneficiary and stands at the end as the paraclete who must carry on in the spirit he has inherited from McMurphy. Bromden occupies, then, the spiritual center of Kesey's narrative and is thus appropriately its spokesman.

8
POINT OF VIEW

While Kesey was serving as an aide at the Menlo Park Veteran's Hospital and working on a first draft of *Cuckoo's Nest*, he corresponded regularly with Ken Babbs. The letters were a sharing of news and confidences between good friends, but they almost always included an exchange of ideas about the craft of writing fiction. In one of the letters, Kesey revealed the great value he places on point of view:

> I'll discuss point of view for a time now. I am beginning to agree with Stegner, that it truely [sic] is the most important problem in writing. The book I have been doing on the lane [*Cuckoo's Nest/Perry Lane*] is a third person work, but something was lacking; I was not free to impose my perception and bizarre eye on the god-author who is supposed to be viewing the scene, so I tried something that will be extremely difficult to pull off, and, to my knowledge, has never been tried before—the narrator is going to be a character. He will not take part in the action, or ever speak as I, but he will be a character to be influenced by the events that take place, he will have a position and personality, and a character that is not essentially mine (though it may, by chance, be).[46]

As the novel took shape, this original conception evolved into the character of Bromden, who does have to speak as "I" but who functions as the Kesey persona once removed and whose detachment from the action and the dramatic speech is accomplished by his feigned deafness and dumbness and his real schizophrenia. The curious result of this point of view is a character that is both in and out of the action.

BROMDEN AS SAYER

For there are really two Bromdens in the novel. One is the narrator-participant, who opens the novel in the ward with the scared comment, "They're out there"(9), and who relives his experiences through an unconventionally re-created historical present. This Bromden thinks of himself as "little," fears everything, escapes into his fog, touchingly enters the pastoral painting on the wall to distance himself from ridicule, and reports his distorted but detached perceptions with a sharpness made keen by pain. To this fearful, schizoid figure, time races or drags according to the whims of the Big Nurse in the glass-enclosed station, staff meetings can become orgies of actual blood-letting, a Catholic nurse mortifies her flesh with a steel brush, and the basement of the hospital is full of robotic functionaries and demonic machinery for body disposal. His subjective distortions carry the weight of impressionistic truth, and the time he records is a Dramatic Now.

The other Bromden is the narrator-observer, who is aware of his role as narrator and whose time is a retrospective and reflective Analytical Now. This Bromden frequently detaches himself from the action to comment on himself and others, as in the fishing scene: "I watched, part of them, laughing with them—and somehow not with them. I was off the boat, blown up off the water and skating the wind with those black birds, high above myself, and I could look down and see myself and the rest of the guys"(212). At other times, he reflects deliberately on the turns his tale takes: "I've given what happened next a good lot of thought, and I've come around to thinking that it was bound to be and would have happened in one way or another . . ."(260). As narrator-participant, Bromden is intimidated by people and events, and he operates out of an erratic contact with a shifting reality. As narrator-observer, Bromden maintains a fairly stable narrative identity apart from the dramatic events he recounts and remains involved in as psychologically withdrawn participant. It is a tricky point of view—and a risky one—for if Bromden's bifurcated narrative is too contrived or too incredible, the novel fails.

The novel does not fail, however, because the splintered point of view that Kesey employed grew naturally from the splintered character of the narrator he chose:

> Chief Broom. The very one. From the point of view of craft, Chief Broom was his great inspiration. If he had told the story through McMurphy's eyes, he would have had to end up with the big bruiser delivering a lot of homilies about his down-home theory of mental therapy. Instead, he told the story through the Indian. This way he could present a schizophrenic state the way the schizophrenic himself, Chief Broom, feels it and at the same time report the McMurphy Method more subtly.[47]

And how does the world appear to the consciousness of an institutionalized schizophrenic half-breed Indian with a poetic sensibility? Fragmented. Distorted. Surreal. Painfully vivid. Whether Bromden speaks as narrator-participant in the Dramatic Now or as narrator-observer in the Analytical Now—and these distinctions are sometimes blurred as he works his way toward clarity—he always presents his hypersensitive perceptions with the voice of a poet. His tendency to rhyme has already been noted, but his narrative goes well beyond that formal device. He "translates the unseen into the seen, the abstract into the concrete, giving the Nurse's hatred or the patients' frustrations palpable, visible form."[48]

Bromden's observations, whether distorted or detached, are essentially poetic. He has the power of description that characterizes the sayer and the special vision that characterizes the seer. His sentences are vivid with image, metaphor, simile, and analogy, rhythmical with meter, sometimes roughly harmonized with rhyme, and expansive with symbol. He remembers his father, for example, as "hard and shiny as a gunstock," whereas McMurphy, his hero and surrogate father, is "hard in a different kind of way from Papa, kind of the way a baseball is hard under the scuffed leather"(16). Fellow chronics appear to Bromden as society's battered wrecks, moving toward demolition and often found "bleeding rust in some vacant lot"(19). The young dog in the wet grass moves around "like a fish" and then shakes off spray "in the moon like silver scales" (142). Bromden sympathetically describes Sefelt's head hitting "the tile with a crack like rocks under water" during an epileptic seizure, after which he "melts limp all over the floor in a gray puddle"(152). On the trip to the coast, Bromden sees birds as emblematic of the condition of the inmates worrying over their fetters and their flight toward freedom: "the pigeons fretted up and down the sidewalk with their hands folded behind their backs"(202) and "there was little brown birds occasionally on the fence; when a puff of leaves would hit the fence the birds would fly off with the wind. It looked at first like the leaves were hitting the fence and turning into birds and flying away"(199). Synecdoche is also prominent as a poetic element, and here Bromden, who is not conscious of his poetic devices, serves as Kesey's visionary sensibility in the perception, articulation, and embodiment of the thematic progress from fragmentation to wholeness.

Bromden as Seer

Focusing with his fragmented vision on laughs, hands, faces, Bromden as partial man and synecdochist works his way toward completeness of character and vision and thus validation of Kesey's thesis that broken men—however frightened, beleaguered, splintered, and dehumanized—can be restored to manhood and wholeness. Although Bromden reports much of the story out of his personal fog, he testifies that in the fog parts are especially revealing because "your eyes were working so hard to see in that fog that when something did come in sight every detail was ten times as clear as usual"(116). The clarity of parts eventually leads Bromden—and the novel—to the clarification of wholes.

Bromden perceives the sound and significance of laughter, for example, with a special sensitivity. He flinches psychically in the presence of negative laughter. Public Relation laughs constantly and mindlessly: "Public Relation's shirt collar is so tight it bloats his face up when he laughs, and he's laughing most of the time I don't know what at, laughing high and fast like he wishes he could stop but can't do it"(37). His is the laughter of the compulsive who must disguise with fraudulent cheerfulness the fundamental dishonesty of his public function. The black aides belittle Bromden—"Big enough to eat apples off my head an' he mine me like a baby"(9)—and laugh hatefully: "They laugh and then I hear them mumbling behind me . . . humming hate and death and other hospital secrets"(10). The service station attendants laugh at the notion that the fishing expedition is a "work crew": "Both of the guys laughed. I could tell by the laugh that they'd decided to sell us the gas . . . but it didn't make me feel any better"(200). Bromden and the others are similarly hurt by the derisive laughter they are the objects of on the docks, where "a bunch of loafers" were "making comments and sniggering and goosing one another in the ribs"(205). Bromden begins to feel so worthless that he slips into the pathetic fallacy and imagines even nonhuman elements ridiculing them: "The wind was blowing the boats at their moorings, nuzzling them up against the wet rubber tires along the dock so they made a sound like they were laughing at us. The water was giggling under the boards"(205). Unhealthy laughter is a mocking weapon, cutting sensitive spirits like Bromden to the quick.

Intimidation of this nature imposes on the vulnerable a deathly silence, the clutch of the Combine at the throat. Bromden's total withdrawal from social intercourse gives mute testimony to the power of such intimidation, and he imagines how it begins in others with his poignant scenario of the little boy in the schoolyard who is forever cracked off the end of the whip into the fence in a symbolic game of crack-the-whip. All the other five thousand kids are a part of the whip and thus unidentifiable and interchangeable in the identical five thousand houses. The cracked-off kid is identifiable by his bruises and lacerations and thus does not fit in anywhere: "He wasn't able to open up and laugh either. It's a hard thing to laugh if you can feel the pressure of those beams coming from every new car that passes, or every new house you pass"(204). The problem is the same in the ward, where Bromden sees a kind of "cartoon world . . . that might be real funny if it weren't for the cartoon figures being real guys . . ."(34). In the ward, Big Nurse actively discourages laughter. She never laughs herself, and "She has the ability to turn her smile into whatever expression she wants to use on somebody, but the look she turns it into is no different, just a calculated and mechanical expression to serve her purpose"(47).

The inability to laugh, therefore, is both a gauge of the Combine's pressure and, ironically, a tipped scale of psychic imbalance. "Man, when you lose your laugh," says McMurphy, "you lose your *footing*"(65). In the cuckoo's nest, Bromden is surrounded by a ward full of men who have lost their footing. For twenty years Bromden has been confined in rooms where he feels "the air is pressed in by the walls, too tight for laughing. There's something strange about a place where the men won't let themselves loose and laugh"(48). Even the impulse to laugh has been stifled: "They tell jokes to each other and snicker in their fists (nobody ever dares let loose and laugh . . .)"(19). McMurphy, though, enters the ward and Bromden's consciousness laughing, with a laugh that "spreads in rings bigger and bigger till it's lapping against the walls all over the ward"(16). Calling it "real" and the first laugh he has "heard in years," Bromden identifies the sound with the character: "Even when he isn't laughing, that laughing sound hovers around him, the way the sound hovers around a big bell just quit ringing"(16). Such laughter is free, natural, healthy, honest, and celebrative, and through McMurphy's magnetism, it becomes contagious, but the process is long and difficult.

The fear and silence induced by the humorless Big Nurse has to contend with McMurphy's countertherapy of liberating laughter. On McMurphy's second day in the ward, Bromden watches the newcomer "being the clown, working at getting some of the guys to laugh. It bothers him that the best they can do is grin weakly and snigger sometimes"(92). Later Bromden notes that McMurphy would "Whack his leg and throw back his head and laugh and laugh, digging his thumb into the ribs of whoever was sitting next to him, trying to get him to

laugh too"(139). McMurphy's therapy and the laughter motif culmi-
nate in the climactic fishing scene. Here at last the men, escaping all
derision and pressure, achieve the humanizing laughter McMurphy
has labored so hard to teach them. McMurphy's healing laughter that
initially was "lapping against the walls all over the ward," is here mul-
tiplied by his twelve disciples and cast on the waters—"a laughter that
rang out on the water in ever-widening circles, farther and farther,
until it crashed up on beaches all over the coast, on beaches all over
all coasts, in wave after wave after wave"(212). As usual, Bromden
reports this scene of transformation in hyperbole, but in contrast to
most of his other exaggerations, this one is affirmative and celebrative.
Amid the sound of newly created and now unified laughter, Bromden
experiences an inspiring power and visualizes the tidal force of freedom, fellowship, and love washing incessantly against the universal
shores of absurdity. Despite his hyperbole, however, he keeps his balance and retains the explicit moral of McMurphy's lesson: "you have
to laugh at the things that hurt you just to keep yourself in balance,
just to keep the world from running you plumb crazy"(212).

From this point until his death, McMurphy maintains his laughter with increasing difficulty, but his persistence stamps on the growing
awareness of Bromden the existential nature of heroic resistance: "The
thing he was fighting, you couldn't whip it for good. All you could do
was keep on whipping it, till you couldn't come out any more and
somebody else had to take your place"(265). The boxing metaphor
that Bromden uses here implies that he himself will be the new contender against the Combine, and it emphasizes the importance of
hands, another synecdoche that Bromden is sensitive to in his movement toward wholeness. Like the laughter motif, the hands motif is
introduced with the admission of McMurphy to the ward. Greeting
silence with laughter, he grasps weak hands with strong ones.

Bromden notes with the eyes of a fellow-sufferer the afflictions of
the men conveyed by their hands. George Sorenson, the big Swede,
paranoiacally keeps his hands to himself, fearing the polluting touch
of others. Harding has expressive hands, "free as two white birds,"
but he is ashamed of his effeminacy and therefore "traps them between

his knees; it bothers him that he's got pretty hands"(23). In his stance of terrified crucifixion, Ellis cannot move even to the latrine "before the nails pull his hands back to the wall"(25). The guilt-ridden Pilate figure on Disturbed ceaselessly tries to "wash [his] hands of the whole deal"(232). Pete Bancini manages only once to overcome his mortal fatigue and strike a mighty blow but then "his iron ball shrank back to a hand"(52). To these needy ones, McMurphy offers the helping hand of friendship to counteract the debilitating influence of Big Nurse, whose hand affects most of them as it affects Mr. Taber: "The Big Nurse . . . locked her hand on his arm, paralyzes him all the way to the shoulder"(35).

Thus when McMurphy extends the hand of friendship to the men in the cuckoo's nest, he encounters the fleshly evidence of seemingly hopeless debility: "He shakes the hands of Wheelers and Walkers and Vegetables, shakes hands that he has to pick up out of laps like picking up dead birds, mechanical birds, wonders of tiny bones and wires that have run down and fallen"(25). The hand that McMurphy presents is thrust into Bromden's fog with the impact of an illuminated painting:

> I remember real clear the way that hand looked: there was carbon under the fingernails where he'd worked once in a garage; there was an anchor tattooed back from the knuckles; there was a dirty Band-Aid on the middle knuckle, peeling up at the edge. All the rest of the knuckles were covered with scars and cuts, old and new. I remember the palm was smooth and hard as bone from hefting the wooden handles of axes and hoes, not the hand you'd think could deal cards. The palm was callused, and the calluses were cracked, and dirt was worked up in the cracks. A road map of his travels up and down the West. (27)

The effect of McMurphy's handshake contrasts sharply with the paralyzing touch of Big Nurse's hand. Bromden remembers his "fingers were thick and strong closing over mine, and my hand commenced to feel peculiar and went to swelling up out there on my stick of an arm, like he was transmitting his own blood into it. It rang with blood and power"(27). Inspired by McMurphy's audacious challenge to Big

Nurse, the men begin to emulate him: " 'You're *betting* on this?' Cheswick is hopping from foot to foot and rubbing his hands together like McMurphy rubs his"(68). Big Nurse accurately calls McMurphy a "manipulator"(29), but his manipulations lead toward manhood and not, as Big Nurse infers, to self-aggrandizement.

The hands motif climaxes in the second TV vote, when McMurphy calls on the men to show some semblance of manhood: "I want to see the hands," he says, "I want to see the hands that don't go up, too"(124). Retreating to the safety of his fog, Bromden reports the first hand signals of manhood's timorous entry into the ward:

> The first hand that comes up, I can tell, is McMurphy's. . . . And then off down the slope I see them, other hands coming up out of the fog. It's like . . . that big red hand of McMurphy's is reaching into the fog and dropping down and dragging the men up by their hands, dragging them blinking into the open. First one, then another, then the next. Right on down the line of Acutes, dragging them out of the fog till there they stand, all twenty of them, raising not just for watching TV, but against the Big Nurse, against her trying to send McMurphy to Disturbed, against the way she's talked and acted and beat them down for years. (124)

At last, Bromden, too, lifts his hand: "McMurphy's got hidden wires hooked to it, lifting it slow just to get me out of the fog. He's doing it, wires . . . No. That's not the truth. I lifted it myself"(126). The Chief's vote makes twenty-one, "a majority," significant here as the legal age of manhood and the winning hand in blackjack. The seeds of manhood are sown here with this show of hands, defiance, and returning courage. They fructify, with laughter, in the fishing scene, when the men seek McMurphy's helping hand but discover when he withholds his help the resourcefulness of their own hands instead.

Beyond the laughter and the hands, Bromden as Kesey's synecdochist is compelled by the significance of faces, and a survey of his perceptions reveals from another angle the evolution of McMurphy's heroism and its shift to Bromden. In the ward, Bromden painfully examines the faces of victims. Framed by his fog, these faces show their anguish to Bromden starkly, as though, he claims, he were looking through "one of those microscopes"(12):

> I see a Chronic float into sight a little below me. It's old Colonel Matterson, reading from the wrinkled scripture of that long yellow hand. . . . His face is enormous, almost more than I can bear. . . . The face is sixty years of southwest Army camps, rutted by iron-rimmed caisson wheels, worn to the bone by thousands of feet on two-day marches . . .
>
> There's old Pete, face like a searchlight. . . . He tells me once about how tired he is, and just his saying it makes me see his whole life on the railroad . . . doing his absolute damnedest to keep up with a job that comes so easy to the others. . . .
>
> Here comes Billy Bibbit. . . . His face is out to me like the face of a beggar, needing so much more'n anybody can give. . . .
>
> Put your face away, Billy.
>
> They keep filing past.
>
> It's like each face was a sign like one of those "I'm Blind" signs the dago accordian players in Portland hung around their necks, only these signs say "I'm tired" or "I'm scared" or "I'm dying of a bum liver" or "I'm all bound up with machinery and people *pushing* me alla time." I can read all the signs, it don't make any difference how little the print gets. . . . The faces blow past in the fog like confetti. (119–22)

Bromden can read the signs—and does so with poetic intensity—but he cannot help. "None of us can," he thinks in weakness and despair. "You got to understand that as soon as a man goes to help somebody, he leaves himself wide open"(121). McMurphy comes to prove Bromden only half right: commitment to others does leave one vulnerable, but help is possible; something can be done. McMurphy rises to the challenges presented by these human faces of need and by the nonhuman face of Big Nurse, "smooth, calculated, and precision-made"(11) proclaiming the formidable power of the Combine. Public Relation documents that power in another way: "He never, never looks at the men's faces . . ."(38).

The stages of McMurphy's developing heroism are captured in the faces. His compassion is engaged by Harding, whose "face is tilted oddly, edged, jagged purple and gray, a busted wine bottle"(60), by Pete's tired face, Ruckly's burnt-out one, Billy's beggar's face, Cheswick's macho mask, the "faces all round . . . trapped screaming behind mirrors"(12). McMurphy is brought back from his temporary withdrawal by the "canceled row of faces"(150) that look away from him when he fails to support Cheswick, by Cheswick's drowned face, Sefelt's seizure-torn face, and the faces Martini calls to his attention: "Hold it a minute. They need you to see thum"(161). McMurphy signals his return to the championing of the men's cause by driving his fist through the glass of the Nurses' Station and leaving Big Nurse "with her face shifting and jerking"(173).

From this point on, Bromden notices the increasing contrast between the two faces of McMurphy, between the fearless face of the hero he presents to inspire the men and the exhausted face of overextended man he tries to keep hidden from them as he pays the price of superhuman heroism. The laughing face of the triumphant fisher of men is balanced against the fatigued face of the "dedicated lover" reflected in the windshield, whose face is "dreadfully tired and strained and *frantic,* like there wasn't time left for something he had to do . . ."(218). McMurphy's sense of messianic urgency is kept alive daily because "that circle of faces waits and watches"(236). Repeated shock treatments do not alter his resistance nor reduce his defiance: "aware that everyone of those faces on Disturbed had turned toward him and was waiting . . . he'd tell the nurse he regretted he had but one life to give for his country and she could kiss his rosy red ass before he'd give up the goddam ship"(242). McMurphy valiantly continues his resistance despite the fact that after each shock treatment Bromden can see "his whole face drained of color, looking thin and scared"(243) until the final depletion that brings on his death: "There's nothin' in the face"(269). Having "doled out his life"(218) for others to live, he has emptied his own.

Bromden is now prepared, however, to carry on where McMurphy has left off, and returning from Disturbed, he begins to feel for the first time the pressure that the weak can exert on the strong: "Everybody's face turned up to me with a different look than they'd ever given me before. . . . I grinned back at them, realizing how McMurphy must've felt these months with these faces screaming up at him"(243). As a fragmented man grown whole in McMurphy's image, Bromden has become strong enough to assume responsibility for killing his friend and heroic model, courageous enough to liberate himself with the control panel amid a "baptizing" of splintered glass, heading in the direction of the dog and geese, "flying free," compassionate enough to go home "to see if there's any of the guys . . . back in the village who haven't drunk themselves goofy"(272). His aim is to minister to the faces of need, to extend the range of heroism.

Bromden's final act of courage is to relive his experience honestly and tell it truthfully despite the pain it causes. At the outset, Bromden as narrator-observer calls attention to the retrospective re-creative duality of his narration and to the complicated nature of its reliability:

> It's gonna burn me . . . finally telling about all this, about the hospital, and her, and the guys—and about McMurphy. I been silent so long now it's gonna roar out of me like floodwaters and you think the guy telling this is ranting and raving my *God*; you think this is too horrible to have really happened, this is too awful to be the truth! But, please. It's still hard for me to have a clear mind thinking on it. But it's the truth even if it didn't happen. (13)

This statement ends the first chapter, but it fits chronologically with Bromden's admission at the end, "I been away a long time"(272), for both comments come from Bromden as narrator-observer looking over his own narrative re-creation of his experiences as narrator-participant. In the process of telling about his experiences, he necessarily relives them, and he reports the nature of his life in the hospital exactly as he recalls it in an exercise of psychic ordering. To articulate his experience is to possess it and, in some measure, to control it. His observation that "it's the truth even if it didn't happen" is not an admission that his narrative is the raving of a madman, but the acknowledgment that he cannot always sort out in the "floodwaters" of memory and impression the actual from the hallucinatory, the real from the surreal. Both were true to his experience, and he wishes to report them as he lived them in his movement from fragmentation to wholeness, from Chronic to man.

The salvation through love that Kesey has presented in *Cuckoo's Nest* seems genuinely possible, despite the pervading cynicism of the modern age, because Kesey has shown its effects dramatically and convincingly in the evolution of McMurphy and the transformation of Bromden, who serves so eloquently as the spokesman and integrating principle in the novel. Although moving and sad, the death of McMurphy is realistic and necessary to document at once the forces of oppression and fear and the power of love to overcome such forces. The novel ends not on the tragic loss of McMurphy's life but on the reclamation through McMurphy's sacrifice of the lives of others, especially Bromden's. The affirmation in the final tone of the novel is earned in the psychical distance Bromden travels from sickness to health and in the verisimilitude of the narrative vehicle that records the journey. Although Bromden as narrator never claims to be a poet, his perceptions reflect the intensity of a poetic sensibility and are embodied in concretions organically related to character and theme. His chosen role as deaf-mute observer removes him from active life, but it makes him an attentive and reliable witness—even when he is in his fog, he reports it reliably—and thus lends vividness to his images appropriate to his function as seer. His early attraction to rhyme expresses itself as a rhyming movement toward reason. His hyperbole, impressionism, and surrealism document both this paranoia and the distortion of values and people in the world he perceives. His transformation from fragmented patient to whole man is captured in his splintered yet almost systematic examination of those isolated parts of other men that reflect his own fragmentation: laughs, hands, faces. This synecdoche is a significant dimension of his progression to wholeness, as is his exchange of the microcosmic ward for the macrocosmic outside world. His spiritual renascence, verbal resourcefulness, and heroic resolve at the end project a poetic response to the possibilities of life. That other data might be adduced to challenge Kesey's vision sociologically or other more negative philosophical conclusions drawn from evidence that he presents does not vitiate in any way the power of the literary affirmation that Kesey achieves through the pairing of McMurphy and Bromden in a fully realized fictive embodiment of the triumph of the most ennobling impulses in the human spirit over the most dehumanizing ones.

NOTES

1. Tony Tanner, *City of Words: American Fiction 1950–1970* (New York: Harper & Row, 1971), 15.

2. Josephine Hendin, *Vulnerable People: A View of American Fiction Since 1945* (New York: Oxford University Press, 1979), 6.

3. Ken Kesey, *Kesey's Garage Sale* (New York: Viking Press, 1973), 7.

4. David Galloway, *The Absurd Hero in American Fiction: Updike, Styron, Bellow, Salinger,* rev. ed. (Austin: University of Texas Press, 1981), xiii.

5. John W. Hunt, introduction to "Perspectives on a Cuckoo's Nest: A Symposium on Ken Kesey," in *Lex et Scientia* 13, nos. 1 and 2 (January–March 1977):7.

6. Terence Martin, "*One Flew Over the Cuckoo's Nest* and the High Cost of Living," *Modern Fiction Studies* 19, no. 1 (Spring 1973):46.

7. Robert Forrey, "Ken Kesey's Psychopathic Savior: A Rejoinder," *Modern Fiction Studies* 21 (Summer 1975):224.

8. Terry G. Sherwood, "*One Flew Over the Cuckoo's Nest* and the Comic Strip," *Critique* 13, no. 1 (1970):100.

9. John Wilson Foster, "Hustling to Some Purpose: Kesey's *One Flew Over the Cuckoo's Nest,*" *Western American Literature* 9 (Summer 1974):126.

10. William J. Handy, "Chief Bromden: Kesey's Existentialist Hero," *North Dakota Quarterly* 48, no. 4 (Autumn 1980):73.

11. For a reading of the novel as a tragedy, see Michael M. Boardman, "*One Flew Over the Cuckoo's Nest*: Rhetoric and Vision," *Journal of Narrative Technique* 9 (1979):171–83.

12. Bruce Carnes, *Ken Kesey* (Boise, Idaho: Boise State University, 1974), 6.

13. Barry H. Leeds, *Ken Kesey* (New York: Frederick Ungar Publishing Co., 1981), 13–14.

14. M. Gilbert Porter, *The Art of Grit: Ken Kesey's Fiction* (Columbia: University of Missouri Press, 1982), 9.

15. Stephen L. Tanner, *Ken Kesey* (Boston: Twayne Publishers, 1983), 26.

16. Peter O. Whitmer, "Ken Kesey's Search for the American Frontier," *Saturday Review*, May–June 1983, 27.

17. Malcolm Bradbury, *The Modern American Novel* (Oxford: Oxford University Press, 1983), 157.

18. Ken Kesey, *One Flew Over the Cuckoo's Nest* (New York: Signet Books, 1962), 255; hereafter cited in the text.

19. Eudora Welty, "How I Write," *Virginia Quarterly Review* 31 (Winter 1955):242–43.

20. Gordon Lish, "A Celebration of Excellence: Ken Kesey," *Genesis West* 2, no. 5 (Fall 1963):23.

21. Speer Morgan, "Ken Kesey," *AWP Newsletter* 10, no. 6 (October 1981):4.

22. "If we look at each of the stories, Bromden's and McMurphy's, in the context of the other, we see an exchange of visions, a clash between the originally tragic view of Bromden, to which hope has been added, and the hopeful view of McMurphy, which became completely qualified by tragedy from the day he signed on for the whole game. Though each attentuates the vision of the other, Bromden's view remains the larger." John W. Hunt, "Flying the Cuckoo's Nest: Kesey's Narrator as Norm," *Lex et Scientia* 13, no. 1 (January–March 1977):32.

23. "The next day they attempt the impossible and . . . reach their majority, twenty-one, in a second vote on the Series. (Interestingly, one of McMurphy's favorite games is blackjack, or twenty-one. Another, fittingly, is stud poker.)" Martin, "High Cost of Living," 50.

24. [Kesey] "still refuses to admit he knew of Billy Budd's stuttering when he modeled his Billy Bibbit upon Melville's character, and his fiction abounds with enough deadly tweaks at literary tradition that his allusions have given some 'straight' critics fits." John Clark Pratt, "On Editing Kesey: Confessions of a Straight Man," in *Kesey*, ed. Michael Strelow (Eugene, Oregon: Northwest Review Books, 1977), 10.

25. In addition to the articles by Leslie Horst, Michael Boardman, Ter-

Notes

ence Martin, and Robert Forrey (cited above), see Elizabeth E. McMahan, "The Big Nurse as Ratchet: Sexism in Kesey's *Cuckoo's Nest*," *CEA Critic* 37, no. 4 (May 1975):25–27.

26. Ronald Billingsley, "The Artistry of Ken Kesey," Ph.D. diss., University of Oregon, 1971, 22.

27. S. Tanner, *Kesey*, 47.

28. John A. Barseness, "Ken Kesey: The Hero in Modern Dress," *Bulletin of the Rocky Mountain Language Association* 23, no. 1 (March 1969):32.

29. Paul Pintarich, "Still Kesey After All These Years," *The Oregonian*, 24 August 1986, Arts and Entertainment section, 3.

30. Henry Adams, "The Dynamo and the Virgin," in *The Education of Henry Adams* (privately printed in 1907); Leo Marx, *The Machine in the Garden* (New York: Oxford University Press, 1964). Both authors examine the cultural split between science and the humanities, technology and art, materialism and spirit, power and morality.

31. Lish, "A Celebration," 20.

32. Critical opinion differs on the effectiveness of cartoon techniques in the novel; here is a representative example of the negative assessment: "Kesey believes in the comic strip world in spite of himself. This is the moral ground on which critical faultfinding must begin. Kesey has not avoided the dangers of a simplistic aesthetic despite his attempts to complicate it. He forgets that the comic strip world is not an answer to life, but an escape from it. The reader finds Kesey entering that world too uncritically in defense of the Good." Sherwood, "Comic Strip," 109.

33. John C. Pratt, *One Flew Over the Cuckoo's Nest: Text and Criticism* (New York: Viking Press, 1973), ix–x.

34. For an extensive discussion of Bromden's function as rhymer, see Porter, *Art of Grit*, 16–21.

35. Raymond M. Olderman, *Beyond the Waste Land: The American Novel in the Nineteen-Sixties* (New Haven, Conn.: Yale University Press, 1972), 47.

36. Joseph Campbell, *The Hero with a Thousand Faces* (Princeton, N.J.: Princeton University Press, 1972), 30.

37. Ibid., 37.

38. Ibid., 59–60.

39. Ibid., 40.

40. Ibid., 39.

41. Strelow, *Kesey*, 17–18.

42. Leeds, *Kesey*, 29–30.

43. Elaine B. Safer, " 'It's the Truth Even if It Didn't Happen' " Ken Kesey's *One Flew Over the Cuckoo's Nest*," *Literature/Film Quarterly* 5, no. 2 (Spring 1977):140.

44. Ruth H. Brady, "Kesey's *One Flew Over the Cuckoo's Nest,*" *Explicator* 31, no. 6 (February 1973): item 41.

45. Richard B. Hauck examines this aspect of the novel in "The Comic Christ and the Modern Reader," *College English* 31 (February 1970):498–506.

46. "Letter to Ken Babbs: 'Peyote and Point of View,' " in Pratt, *Text and Criticism,* 338–39.

47. Tom Wolfe, *The Electric Kool-Aid Acid Test* (New York: Bantam Books, 1969), 44.

48. Ronald Wallace, *The Last Laugh: Form and Affirmation in the Contemporary American Novel* (Columbia: University of Missouri Press, 1979), 112.

SELECTED BIBLIOGRAPHY

Primary Sources

Novels

One Flew Over the Cuckoo's Nest. New York: Viking Press, 1962.
Sometimes a Great Notion. New York: Viking Press, 1964.
Seven Prayers by Grandma Whittier. A serialized novel appearing irregularly
in *Spit in the Ocean,* a little magazine published by Kesey and his asso-
ciates out of Pleasant Hill, Oregon: no. 1 (Winter 1974), no. 2 (Spring
1976), no. 3 (Fall 1977), no. 4 (Winter 1977), no. 5 (Summer 1979), no.
6 ("The Cassady Issue" 1981); no. 7, when it appears, will contain the
last chapter of the novel—the seventh prayer—and will be the last issue
of the magazine.

Collections

Kesey's Garage Sale. New York: Viking Press, 1973.
Kesey. Edited by Michael Strelow. Eugene, Oregon: Northwest Review Books,
1977.
Demon Box. New York: Viking Penguin Inc., 1986.

Interviews and Profiles

Buddy, George. "Ken Kesey: 10 Years After: 'Both a Lightning Rod and a Seismograph.'" *Oregon Daily Emerald,* 24 January 1973, 6–7, 9.

Gaboriau, Linda. "Ken Kesey: Summing Up the '60's, Sizing Up the '70's." *Crawdaddy,* December 1972, 31–39.

Goodwin, Michael. "The Ken Kesey Movie." *Rolling Stone,* 7 March 1970, 24–33.

Krassner, Paul. "An Impolite Interview with Ken Kesey." *Realist,* May–June 1971, 1, 46–53.

―――. "Kesey's Cuckoo War." *City of San Francisco 9,* no. 24 (23 December 1975):25.

Lish, Gordon. "What the Hell You Looking in Here For, Daisy Mae?: An Interview with Ken Kesey." *Genesis West* 2 (Fall 1963):17–29.

Pintarich, Paul. "Still Kesey After All These Years." *Oregonian,* Arts and Entertainment section, 24 August 1986, 1, 3.

Riley, John. "Bio: Novelist Ken Kesey Has Flown the 'Cuckoo's Nest' and Given Up Tripping for Farming." *People Weekly,* 22 March 1976, 24–28.

Secondary Sources

Books

Carnes, Bruce. *Ken Kesey.* Boise, Idaho: Boise State University, 1974. A pamphlet in the BSU Western Writers Series. Carnes provides general analyses of *Cuckoo's Nest, Sometimes a Great Notion,* and *Kesey's Garage Sale,* plus some biographical information and a selected bibliography.

Leeds, Barry H. *Ken Kesey.* New York: Ungar Publishing Co., 1981. The first published full-length study of Kesey's fiction. Leeds supplies a chronology and a biography and examines with critical acuity *Cuckoo's Nest* (novel, play, and movie), *Sometimes a Great Notion, Kesey's Garage Sale,* and *Seven Prayers by Grandma Whittier.* His conclusion is an informed and balanced assessment of Kesey's talent.

Porter, M. Gilbert. *The Art of Grit: Ken Kesey's Fiction.* Columbia: University of Missouri Press, 1982. Short biography and close explication of the intrareferentiality of themes and forms in the first two novels and the *Demon Box* in the form it had assumed by 1982.

Tanner, Stephen L. *Ken Kesey.* Boston: Twayne Publishers, 1983. A comprehensive examination of Kesey and his major work and the criticism that attends it. Sound interpretations and sensible assessments of both primary and secondary material. Good bibliography.

Selected Bibliography

Dissertation

Billingsley, Ronald G. "The Artistry of Ken Kesey." Ph.D. diss., University of Oregon, 1971. Perceptive formalist analysis of the first two novels.

Chapters of Books

Frank, Robert. "Ken Kesey." In *Fifty Western Writers: A Bio-Bibliographical Sourcebook*, edited by Fred Erisman and Richard Etulain, 246–56. Westport, Conn.: Greenwood Press, 1982. A reliable short biography, a perceptive statement of major themes, a balanced survey of criticism, and a selected bibliography.

Hicks, Jack. "Fiction from the Counterculture: Marge Piercy, Richard Brautigan, Ken Kesey." Chapter 4 in *In the Singer's Temple: Prose Fictions of Barthelme, Gaines, Brautigan, Piercy, Kesey, and Kosinski*. Chapel Hill: University of North Carolina Press, 1981. Heavy emphasis on Kesey's personal life and his status as a revolutionary in the analysis of *Cuckoo's Nest* as countercultural fiction designed to reject quotidian American life and to project or evoke "alternative semi-utopian worlds."

Lindberg, Gary. "Faith on the Run." Chapter 11 in *The Confidence Man in American Literature*. New York: Oxford University Press, 1982. A concise and provocative discussion of *Cuckoo's Nest* in the context of the life of Neal Cassady and the novel *On the Road*. Big Nurse is a doubter who alleviates her skepticism through collectivism. McMurphy is a believer and booster-hero who dies for individuality. Bromden evolves into a con man survivor.

Olderman, Raymond M. "The Grail Knight Arrives: Ken Kesey, *One Flew Over the Cuckoo's Nest*." Chapter 1 in *Beyond the Waste Land: The American Novel in the Nineteen-Sixties*. New Haven, Conn: Yale University Press, 1973. A reading of the novel in terms of waste land imagery, vegetation myths, the Grail Knight, the Chapel Perilous, the Fisher King, the Enchantress, and water symbolism.

Tanner, Tony. "Edge City." Chapter 16 in *City of Words: American Fiction 1950–1970*. New York: Harper & Row, 1971. A discussion of the first two novels in terms of cartoon characterizations and the "dread" in American life and letters of a fixed, externally determined existence versus the "dream" of a free, individually determined existence. Bromden escapes the former, but his relation to the latter remains a direction only, not an achievement. Tanner sees Kesey's third "novel" as his life imitating his art in his antics with the Merry Pranksters, an attempt to incorporate others in his "flow" toward the expanded horizons of Edge City.

Wallace, Ronald. "What Laughter Can Do: Ken Kesey's *One Flew Over the Cuckoo's Nest*." in *The Last Laugh: Form and Affirmation in the Contemporary American Comic Novel*. Columbia: University of Missouri

Press, 1979. A persuasive argument that *Cuckoo's Nest* is not in its fundamental generic form a romance, but a comedy. The struggle between McMurphy and Big Nurse is presented in comic terms, and Bromden's transformation is an embodiment of comic values, including a happy ending.

Articles

Barsness, John A. "Ken Kesey: The Hero in Modern Dress." *Bulletin of the Rocky Mountain Language Association* 23, no. 1 (March 1969):27–33. A short but pithy reading of the first two novels. Perceptive, eloquent, especially good on Kesey's verisimilitude and the American nature of his heroes.

Beards, Richard D. "Stereotyping in Modern American Fiction: Some Solitary Swedish Madmen." *Moderna Språk* 63, no. 4 (1969):329–37. Examines the stereotypical Swede in several American novels, including *One Flew Over the Cuckoo's Nest*. George Sorenson (Rub-a-dub) fits the stereotype because of his fishing background, his linguistic inflections, his solitariness, and his mania for cleanliness.

Beidler, Peter G., and John W. Hunt. "Perspectives on a Cuckoo's Nest: A Symposium on Ken Kesey." In *Lex et Scientia, The International Journal of Law and Science* 13, nos. 1 & 2 (January–March 1977). Two issues of the journal combined for a special exploration of issues in *Cuckoo's Nest* from interdisciplinary perspectives. Included are "Facing Things Honestly: McMurphy's Conversion," Jack DeBellis; "Bitches, Twitches, and Eunuchs: Sex-Role Failure and Caricature," Leslie Horst; "Ken Kesey's Indian Narrator: A Sweeping Stereotype?," Peter G. Beidler; "The Forces of Fear: Anatomy of Insanity," Annette Benert; "Flying the Cuckoo's Nest: Kesey's Narrator as Norm," John W. Hunt; "A Place Apart: The Historical Context of Kesey's Asylum," Robert Rosenwin; "Machine, Mops, and Medicaments: Therapy in the Cuckoo's Nest," Roger C. Loeb; "Regaining Freedom: Sanity in Insane Places," Ellen Herrenkohl; "From Folded Hands to Clenched Fists: Kesey and Science Fiction," Edward J. Gallagher; "Of Beats and Beasts: Power and the Individual in the Cuckoo's Nest," Robert Rosenwein; "From Rabbits to Men: Self-Reliance in the Cuckoo's Nest," Peter G. Beidler; "Art and Ideology: Kesey's Approach to Fiction," Addison C. Bross; "Everything Running Down: Ken Kesey's Vision of Imminent Entropy," Joan Bischoff; "Alone No More: Dualisms in American Literary Thought," Jack DeBellis; "From Tragicomedy to Melodrama: The Novel Onstage," Elizabeth Fifer; "Control by Camera: Milos Forman as Subjective Narrator," George B. MacDonald; "The Rules of the Game: Milos Forman's American Allegory," George B. MacDonald; a bibliography is also included (cited elsewhere in this bibliography).

Selected Bibliography

Billingsley, Ronald G., and James W. Palmer. "Milos Forman's *Cuckoo's Nest*: Reality Unredeemed." *Studies in the Humanities* 7, no. 1 (December 1978): 14–18. A careful and informed discussion of why the film, though successful as entertainment, fails to realize the novel's themes or Kesey's vision.

Boardman, Michael M. "*One Flew Over the Cuckoo's Nest*: Rhetoric and Vision." *Journal of Narrative Technique* 9 (1979): 171–83. A valuable description of the novel as tragedy and a useful discussion of the issue of sexism, which Boardman sees as a false charge resulting from a failure to distinguish between ideas that really represent Kesey's articles of faith and those elements that are parts of the novel's rhetoric of significant fabulation.

Fiedler, Leslie A. "The New Mutants." *Partisan Review* 32, no. 4 (Fall 1965): 505–29. Fiedler sees Bromden as the "ideal new culture hero" of the post-modern emergence of mutants who pursue vision through hallucination rather than through logic.

Foster, John Wilson. "Hustling to Some Purpose: Kesey's *One Flew Over the Cuckoo's Nest*." *Western American Literature* 9 (Summer 1974): 115–29. Kesey is a hustler who uses Christian symbolism, myth, music-hall pathos, barroom anecdotage, and comic-strip vulgarity to achieve moments of poetry and a qualified affirmation.

Handy, William J. "Chief Bromden: Kesey's Existentialist Hero." *North Dakota Quarterly* 48, no. 4 (1980):72–82. A character study in the context of existential philosophy. Bromden's gradual coming to awareness, his assumption of responsibility for his individual actions, and his commitment to life over death qualify him as an existential hero.

Hoge, James O. "Psychedelic Stimulation and the Creative Imagination: The Case of Ken Kesey." *Southern Humanities Review* 6 (1972): 381–91. A criticism of Kesey for allowing experimentation with drugs to vitiate the lasting quality of his art.

Kunz, Don R. "Mechanistic and Totemistic Symbolism in Kesey's *One Flew Over the Cuckoo's Nest*." *Studies in American Fiction* 3 (Spring 1975): 65–82. An examination of the conflict between the mechanism of the Combine and the vitalistic totemism of McMurphy as seen through the Indian eyes and experience of schizophrenic Bromden. Excellent tracing of the bird imagery in the novel. McMurphy becomes Bromden's mythical guardian spirit.

Martin, Terence. "*One Flew Over the Cuckoo's Nest* and the High Cost of Living." *Modern Fiction Studies* 19, no. 1 (Spring 1973): 43–55. A solid discussion of the emasculating-woman theme, the characterization of McMurphy, and the definition of manhood and humanity. Living free exacts a high toll, a cost that McMurphy pays and that Bromden finds the courage to face.

Mills, Nicholas. "Ken Kesey and the Politics of Laughter." *Centennial Review* 16 (Winter 1972):82–90. With his two principal characters, Kesey reverses the myth of the Indian introducing the white man to the natural life. McMurphy's politics teach that laughter is not intended to eliminate failure and death but that failure and death do not have to be deterrents to action and a full life.

McMahan, Elizabeth E. "The Big Nurse as Ratchet: Sexism in Kesey's *Cuckoo's Nest*." *CEA Critic* 37, no. 4 (May 1975): 25–27. A short article castigating Kesey for the dehumanized depiction of Big Nurse.

Pearson, Carol. "The Cowboy Saint and the Indian Poet: The Comic Hero in Kesey's *One Flew Over the Cuckoo's Nest*." *Studies in American Humor* 1 (October 1974): 91–98. A brief study of character and genre and Kesey's idiosyncratic transformation of both.

Sherman, W. D. "The Novels of Ken Kesey." *Journal of American Studies* 5 (1971):185–96. A speculation that *Cuckoo's Nest* and *Sometimes a Great Notion* are emblematic of hallucinatory drug experiences.

Sherwood, Terry G. "*One Flew Over the Cuckoo's Nest* and the Comic Strip." *Critique* 13, no. 1 (1971): 96–109. An excellent explication of *Cuckoo's Nest* in terms of Kesey's use of popular culture, especially the comic strip. Sherwood's final evaluation is that McMurphy is so tied to the delimiting caricature that his humanism is not convincing and thus the book falls victim to its own controlling device. This article raises a number of important issues.

Sullivan, Ruth. "Big Mama, Big Papa, and Little Sons in Ken Kesey's *One Flew Over the Cuckoo's Nest*." *Literature and Psychology* 25 (1975):33–44. A Freudian reading of the novel in terms of the Oedipus complex.

Valentine, Virginia. "Kesey's *One Flew Over the Cuckoo's Nest*." *Explicator* 41, no. 1 (Fall 1982):58–59. Pessimistic interpretation of the ending of the novel based on Christian parallels and internal image clusters.

Waldmeir, Joseph. "Two Novelists of the Absurd: Heller and Kesey." *Wisconsin Studies in Contemporary Literature* 5 (1964):192–204. A penetrating comparison of *Catch-22* to *Cuckoo's Nest*. Waldmeir finds Kesey's novel superior because he achieves greater unity and because he is unwilling to throw his people away for mere comic effect, as Heller characteristically does.

———. "Only an Occasional Rutabaga: American Fiction Since 1945," *Modern Fiction Studies* 15 (Winter 1969–70):467–81. This essay classifies American fiction since 1945 in five categories and discusses Kesey along with nine other "quest" novelists. In *Cuckoo's Nest*, the motivating force behind the quest is love, which inspires McMurphy's sacrifice and Bromden's subsequent growth to full humanity.

Wallis, Bruce E. "Christ in the Cuckoo's Nest: Or, the Gospel According to Ken Kesey." *Cithara* 12 (1972):52–58. Wallis finds McMurphy's gospel of vital sexuality too simplistic as a way of coping with the complex realities of evil.

Wildmer, Kingsley. "The Post-Modernist Art of Protest: Kesey and Mailer as American Expressions of Rebellion." *Centennial Review* 19 (Summer

1975):121–35. A comparison of Kesey and Mailer as two writers who live, think, and write in the Hemingway tradition of supermasculinity and whose work, therefore, contains homoerotic motifs and misogynistic themes and characters. Widmer praises Kesey's aesthetic coherence but decries the misogynistic colorations he perceives in Kesey's work, particularly in *Cuckoo's Nest*.

Bibliographies

Bischoff, Joan. "Views and Reviews: An Annotated Bibliography." *Lex et Scientia* 13, nos. 1 & 2 (1977):93–103. The most inclusive Kesey bibliography in print on *Cuckoo's Nest*.

Weixlmann, Joseph. "Ken Kesey: A Bibliography." *Western American Literature* 10 (1975):219–31. Covers *Cuckoo's Nest, Sometimes a Great Notion*, and *Kesey's Garage Sale*. Although twelve years old now, this is still the most comprehensive bibliography on Kesey's work available.

INDEX

Index

faces motif, 100
Falk, Marcia L., 17, 76
Faulkner, William, 48
Feld, Rose, 16
Ferraro, Geraldine, 8
Fiedler, Leslie: 82; *The Return of the Vanishing American*, 21
"Fighting Leathernecks," 82
Folklore, 82
Ford, Gerald, 6
Forrey, Robert, 20
Foster, John Wilson, 20
Franklin, Aretha, 6
Franklin, Benjamin, 12
Friedan, Betty: *The Feminine Mystique*, 5

Galbraith, John Kenneth: *The Affluent Society*, 3
Gallagher, Edward J., 19
Galloway, David, 13
Goodman, Paul: *Growing Up Absurd*, 5
Grateful Dead, the, 5
Greer, Germaine: *The Female Eunuch*, 7
Guthrie, Woody, 5

hands motif, 98
Handy, William J., 20
Hart, Gary, 9
Hawthorne, Nathaniel, 12
Heavy Metal, 10
Hefner, Hugh, 7
Heller, Joseph: *Catch 22*, 27
Hell's Angels, 82
Hendin, Josephine: 13; *Vulnerable People*, 12
Heraclitus, 56
Hicks, Jack: 21; *In the Singer's Temple: Prose Fictions of Barthelme, Gaines, Brautigan, Piercy, Kesey, and Kosinski*, 22
"Hippies," 7
Hirsch, E. D., Jr.: *Cultural Literacy: What Every American Needs to Know*, 9

Hoffman, Abbie: *Revolution for the Hell of It*, 6
Horst, Leslie, 18
House Committee on Un-American Activities, 3
Hunt, John W., 18, 108n22

The Gay Liberation Front, 5

Iacocca, Lee, 8

James, Henry: 72; "The Art of Fiction," 47
Jefferson Airplane, 5
Jelliffe, R. A., 16
Johnson, Lyndon B., 4
Joyce, James, 85
Jung, C. G., 85

Kafka, Franz, 77, 78
Kennedy, John F., 4, 6
Kennedy, Robert, 6
Kenniston, Kenneth: *The Young Radicals*, 5
Kent State University, 6
Kesey, Ken: 23, 29, 31, 32, 77; *The Demon Box*, 8; Life, 2–10; *One Flew Over the Cuckoo's Nest*, 5, 11, 13, 14, 15, 28, 29, 37, 47, 89, 104; *Sometimes a Great Notion*, 5
Kinsey, Alfred: *Sexual Behavior of the American Male; Sexual Behavior of the American Female*, 3

laughter motif, 95
Leeds, Barry: *Ken Kesey*, 22
Levin, Martin, 16
Lish, Gordon: "A Celebration of Excellence: Ken Kesey," 81
Loeb, Roger C., 19

McFarlane, Robert, 10
McLuhan, Marshall, 1; *Understanding Media*, 5
Malin, Irving, 17

Index

Truman, Harry S., 2
Twain, Mark, 77, 78
Twisted Sister, 10

U. S. Marines, 9

Vietnam, 4, 6, 8

"Wagoner's Lad, The," 79
Wallace, Ronald: *The Last Laugh:
Form and Affirmation in the
Contemporary American Comic
Novel*, 21
Wasserman, Dale, 17
Watergate Scandal, 6
Welty, Eudora: "How I Write," 31
Whitman, Walt, 12
Whitmer, Peter, 23

Whyte, William H.: *The
Organization Man*, 3
Wild Bill Hickok, 82
Wolfe, Tom: "The Me Decade and
the Third Great Awakening," 7
Women's Lib, 5
World War II:
Hiroshima, 2
Japanese-American Relocation
Camps, 2
Nagasaki, 2
Pearl Harbor, 2
See also Truman, Harry S., 2

"Yippies," 7
Young Americans for Freedom, 4
"Yuppies," 8

ABOUT THE AUTHOR

M.Gilbert Porter is a professor of English at the University of Missouri–Columbia, where he teaches contemporary fiction, American literature, and literary criticism. He has received an AMOCO Foundation Award for Distinguished Undergraduate Teaching and was a Fulbright-Hays Professor of American literature in Yugoslavia in 1977–78 and a visiting professor at the University of the Saarland in Saabrücken, West Germany, in 1984. Among his publications are *Whence the Power?: The Artistry and Humanity of Saul Bellow* (1974) and *The Art of Grit: Ken Kesey's Fiction* (1982). When he is not engaged in academic activities, he and his wife, Georgeanne, are striving to convert one hundred and eleven acres of Missouri timberland into a working farm.